THE BULLDOG

Diane Morgan

The Bulldog

Project Team
Editor: Stephanie Fornino
Copy Editor: Jessica White
Indexer: Dianne Schneider
Design: Stephanie Krautheim
Series Design: Mada Design
Series Originator: Dominique De Vito

T.F.H. Publications
President/CEO: Glen S. Axelrod
Executive Vice President: Mark E. Johnson
Publisher: Christopher T. Reggio
Production Manager: Kathy Bontz

T.F.H. Publications, Inc.
One TFH Plaza
Third and Union Avenues
Neptune City, NJ 07753

ISBN 978-0-7938-3631-4

Printed and bound in China
11 12 13 14 15   11 13 14 12

Library of Congress Cataloging-in-Publication Data
Morgan, Diane, 1947 —
The Bulldog / Diane Morgan.
p. cm.
Includes index.
ISBN 0-7938-3631-X (alk. paper)
1. Bulldog. I. Title.
SF459.B85M67 2005
639.72--dc22
2005006632

The Leader In Responsible Animal Care For Over 50 Years!®
www.tfh.com

TABLE OF CONTENTS

HISTORY
of the Bulldog

The Bulldog is one of the world's most universally recognized and beloved breeds. He has long been one of the symbols of Britain, partly because famous "John Bull," the English counterpart of Uncle Sam, looked rather like a Bulldog in a vest, and partly because he is supposed to resemble the English in terms of his determination and courage.

The first description of the Bulldog appeared in 1500, when a certain W. Wulcher referred to the breed as the "Bondogge" in reference to the practice of Bulldogs being tied up (bonded) with other dogs. Shakespeare also mentioned the breed in his play *King Henry VI*, although the actual term "Bulldog" first appeared in writing in 1609. However, it was only in the 1630s that the breed started to look like the present-day Bulldog. Some people call the Bulldog the "English" Bulldog, perhaps as opposed to the French Bulldog or the American Bulldog, but the official name of this breed is simply "Bulldog." Those who admire and own Bulldogs are called Bulldoggers.

REALLY ANCIENT BULLDOG HISTORY

As hard as it may be to believe, once there was a world without Bulldogs, although it wasn't a world any of us would want to live in. (Before there were Bulldogs, there was no central heating. I'm not saying there's a cause and effect relationship here, but it is a fact.)

At any rate, to better know who the Bulldog is, we should take a look at his relatives. Wolves, jackals, foxes, and dogs are all members of the family Canidae, and wolves and dogs are so close as to share the same species name, *Canis lupus*. This means that they can interbreed and have fertile offspring, although left to their own devices, wolves and dogs keep to their own separate communities. They have a different culture and a wildly different outlook on life. Their main difference is philosophic: Dogs like people and wolves don't. Current dogs are descended from certain wolves who had nothing better to do

Bulldogs are mastiff-type dogs who were most likely descended from the Tibetan Mastiff.

than hang around stone-age camp fires hoping for a handout. They must have received them, because modern dogs are still begging for food with roughly equal success.

Bulldogs are mastiff-type dogs, and like all such animals, they are probably descended from the large and dangerous Tibetan Mastiff. How Tibetan Mastiffs arrived in Britain is a mystery. Some speculate that the Phoenicians brought them there, although this is debatable, because the Phoenicians were sailors and Tibet is landlocked. It is probably more accurate to say that the Bulldog's ancestors were the great Molossian Mastiffs. These European war dogs probably owe their heritage to the Tibetan Mastiff somewhere along the line, but the actual line of descent is shrouded in mystery.

The "Sport" of Bullbaiting

It's one of the ironies of history that this noble, gentle breed has a dark past, much of which is tied up in the cruel "sport" of bullbaiting. This activity has its roots in ancient Crete, Greece, and Rome. In those cultures, the bull was actually considered sacred, and a great number of "games" and sacrifices were devised around him. In the beginning, people were used. Later, at least in some locations, dogs took their place. Sometime in the thirteenth century, the Earl Warren, an English lord, happened to notice a group of dogs chasing a bull down the street. He thought it was so amusing that he arranged for the spectacle to be repeated every year six weeks before Christmas.

Between the 13th and 19th centuries, the horrible sports of bull and bearbaiting were spectacles that people of all ages and classes enjoyed. In fact, it was England's most popular sport, and it received government support under King John, one of England's worst kings. (He was so bad that the British never attempted another King John.)

Cattle and dogs have always shared history. Some dog breeds were developed to herd cattle, others to guard them. Bulldogs were bred, at least after a time, to fight them. The first Bulldogs, however, may have been real working dogs whose job was to restrain livestock about to be slaughtered. Eventually, this ugly but perhaps necessary work devolved into a "sport" in which a dog would sneak up on a tethered bull and attempt to grab him by the nose in order to drag him to the ground. The bull, naturally, would defend himself vigorously with his horns. Very often, both combatants would end up dead or seriously injured, which one must suppose was part of the fun. Rules for the "sport" varied from place to place. In one locality, the bull was untethered, and the dog had to pull the bull backward around the ring. In another

National Kennel Clubs

Australia
www.ankc.aust.com

Canada
www.ckc.ca

Denmark
www.dansk-kennel-klub.dk/

Finland
www.kennelliitto.fi/

Japan
www.jkc.or.jp/index_e.html

New Zealand
www.nzkc.org.nz

Norway
www.nkk.no/

Portugal
www.cpc.pt/

Sweden
www.skk.se/

United Kingdom
www.the-kennel-club.org.uk

United States
www.akc.org

The first Bulldogs may have been real working dogs whose main job was to restrain livestock.

The AKC

The American Kennel Club (AKC), founded in 1884, is the most influential dog club in the United States. The AKC is a "club of clubs," meaning that its members are other kennel clubs, not individual people. The AKC registers purebred dogs, supervises dog shows, and is concerned with all dog-related matters, including public education and legislation. It collects and publishes the official standards for all of its recognized breeds.

The United Kingdom version of the AKC is called the Kennel Club. However, the Kennel Club's members are individual persons. The membership of the Kennel Club is restricted to a maximum of 1,500 UK members in addition to 50 overseas members and a small number of honorary life members. The Kennel Club promotes responsible dog ownership and works on important issues like canine health and welfare.

place, the dog was supposed to pin the bull and throw him to the ground while the bull would attempt to disembowel the dog. The handlers tried to catch the thrown dogs, with varying degrees of success. The winning dog was the one who held on the longest. Those who had no saner use for their disposable income bet enormous amounts of money on this "game."

As time went on, it was clear which type of dogs had the best luck against bulls. Mastiffs were used at first, but their large size and off-the-ground stance made them an easy target for the desperate, benighted bulls. The gentlemanly dog whom we know as the Bulldog today was bred down from the Mastiff specifically and solely to participate in this dreadful activity.

The first essential quality was a low-to-the-ground animal, to minimize the chances of the bull's horn being inserted between the dog's belly and the ground. A dog with powerful shoulders and great strength of jaw was obviously required, as well as one with fierce tenacity and the ability to fight on through pain. And if the dog was tossed in the air, it helped to have a short, strong back and less-developed hindquarters to minimize the damage. Good padding around the ribcage helped prevent serious injuries when the animal hit the earth.

Early breeders used all kinds of terrible methods to create the kind of dog they wanted. They encouraged what most people consider deformities and even made puppies wear stiff masks to distort their features even more. They crammed them into kennels with insufficient headroom to force them even lower to the ground. Of course, such body alterations aren't genetically transferable, but early breeders didn't know what kinds of things were inherited and what weren't. They also used torture and cruelty to create a vicious, pain-resistant fighting animal.

The Bulldog's jaw is such an unusual-looking piece of anatomy that it cries out for explanation. The lower jaw, or mandible, extends beyond the front jaw. In most breeds, this is a fault because it truly does interfere with proper chewing. However, it has historic importance. An undershot jaw enabled the Bulldog to grab the bull at any point, clamp down, and hang on. Once the Bulldog got a grip, the jaws "locked." This is not the gentle mouth of a retriever! While hanging on, the animal was still able to breathe, because the nose was set back from the jaw. The Bulldog could actually hang on until the bull bled to death.

Even the wrinkles had a purpose, at least according to some authors. The many folds of the skin permitted the shed blood of the bull to run around the dog's face rather than directly into his eyes. There's also an equally shaky theory that the loose jowls of the Bulldog smothered the bull while the dog was hanging on. It's truer to say that the Bulldog seized the bull by the nostrils and shut off the air supply that way. If you are wondering how your own Bulldog could have managed any of this, it's important to remember that the first Bulldogs were a less exaggerated version of today's models, who usually have to be born by a caesarian section. (The head is the portion of the anatomy to which the most attention is paid in the show ring.)

Bullbaiting was finally made illegal in England in 1835, but it continued underground for many years, just as dog fighting does in the modern world.

THE BULLDOG IN ENGLAND

While the abolition of bullbaiting was a great relief to the bulls and Bulldogs, the breed itself, without an official "use," slowly began to decline. But then something magical happened: the invention of the dog show in the second half of the 19th century. Dog shows were all the excuse aficionados of the breed needed to begin breeding their beloved breed again. However, there was a problem. The first Bulldogs were noble, courageous, and powerful, but they were also incredibly vicious. As a result, breeders were in a quandary. They loved the positive qualities of the breed, but who

Bulldogs at Westminster

The first non-terrier to win Best in Show at Westminster, the oldest organization in the United States committed to the sport of purebred dogs, was a three-year-old Bulldog named Strathtay Prince Albert in 1913. Prince Albert was a British-bred dog who entered the show after arriving in the United States only two weeks before. Prince Albert defeated 200 other Bulldogs to take first prize in Best of Show from a Wire Fox Terrier named Estelle. Estelle is said to have growled at Prince Albert as the white and brindle winner was led away in triumph, and who could blame her? However, Bulldogs had to wait until 1955 to triumph again. In that year, Kippax Fearnought (known as "Jock" to his friends) took the crown. Jock was also an English Bulldog, and his owner had purchased him sight unseen (although to be fair, he did have photos). Jock was justly famous for his gait, described by one observer as that of a "portly old sea captain." *Time* magazine referred to him as a "red and white picture of power when he moved and a stolid, impassive creature when still".

wanted a dog who couldn't be taken out in public?

It dawned on these breeders that whatever use Bulldogs had served in the past was irrelevant. Viciousness had been bred into Bulldogs, and it could be bred out. The premier person responsible for this was Bill George, a breeder who named his kennel the Canine Castle. Other famous early breeders were F.G.W. Crayer, J.S. Pybus Sellon, F.W. Crowther, W.H. Sprague, and A.E. Vicary.

The first written Bulldog standard was drafted in 1864. The Bulldog Club was founded in 1874 and incorporated one year later as the Bulldog Club Inc. This makes the Bulldog Club the oldest breed club in the world. A Standard of Perfection was formulated and published in England in 1875. The club also produces an illustrated magazine twice a year called, simply, *The Bulldog*. The first show for the breed was held in Birmingham, England in 1860. The best of the early Bulldog show animals was a dog with the name of Old King Dick. This dog's genes are present even today in some lines.

The Bulldog Club's stated goals include:

- To promote the breeding of pure Bulldogs of the true type and to urge the adoption of such type upon breeders, judges, committees, and promoters of canine exhibitions.
- To publish and promulgate the true type of pure Bulldogs by means of a standard description of its correct appearance and the various characteristic points in detail of a perfectly formed Bulldog, for uniform adoption as the sole standard of excellence, and for the guidance of breeders and of judges in awarding prizes and distinctions of merit and dog shows or other canine competitions.
- To promote information on canine subjects by means of lectures, discussions, the editing of a journal, books, periodicals, correspondence, drawings, or otherwise.
- To promote, hold, or arrange either independently or in connection with other persons, exhibitions, dog shows and matches, with the object of encouraging the breeding and propagation of the true English Bulldog.
- Another UK club, in some ways established as a rival to the Bulldog Club, is the British Bulldog Club, founded in 1892. Its stated aims are:
- To encourage and promote the breeding of Bulldogs.
- To give prizes, support, and hold exhibitions of Bulldogs.

THE BULLDOG IN
THE UNITED STATES

Bulldogs appear to have been present in America as early as 1774. They were accepted into the American Kennel Club in 1886. The first registered Bulldog was simply named Bob. The Bulldog Club of America was then established in 1890 and incorporated under the laws of the state of New York on February 29, 1904. The framers of its constitution stated its purposes to be as follows:

- To maintain a standard of excellence for the guidance of breeders, owners, and judges.
- To improve the breed through encouragement of effort directed toward approach to, or attainment of, the degree of excellence set forth in the standard of the Bulldog breed.
- To stimulate interest in competitive public showings of Bulldogs.
- To further the interests of the Breed.
- To work for the general good of breeders, owners, and exhibitors of Bulldogs.

Early breeders in the United States include John H. Matthews of New York City, R.B. Sawyer of Milwaukee, E. Sheffield Porter of New Haven, and C.G. Cugle of Hartford. The first Bulldog "show dog" in this country was a fellow named Donald. The first Bulldog to become an American Kennel Club champion was a dog by the name of Robinson Crusoe. He achieved the title in 1888.

One of the most famous Bulldogs in the United States is the brindle and white Sergeant Chesty XI, the official mascot of Marine Barracks Washington D.C. Her "call name" is Molly, which comes from the term "Molly Marines," the name given to the first women in the United States Marine Corps.

The abolition of bullbaiting in 1835 led to the development of the Bulldog as a show dog.

Chapter

CHARACTERISTICS
of the Bulldog

urrently, the Bulldog is one of the most popular breeds of dog. Most people are first drawn to the breed by its unusual appearance and then by its unusual but magnificent character. Both of these attributes need to be examined more closely before you actually plunge into the exciting and wild world of Bulldogdom.

Not everyone, sadly, is Bulldog worthy, and although a lot of people love this breed, the real question is why do you want a Bulldog? With a mug that's ferocious, sour, and comical at the same time and a gait that's powerful and awkward at once, the Bulldog will adore you but will follow his own counsel rather than your commands. He is generally stalwart and strong but at the same time has certain vulnerabilities (mostly related to respiration and stamina) that require special care and some owner indulgence. If you find these traits appealing, then the Bulldog is meant for you!

SUITABILITY OF THE BULLDOG

One of the best ways to find out if a Bulldog is the right dog for you is to look closely at your own personality and lifestyle to see how it fits with the personality, temperament, and physical limitations of this breed.

Are You Status Conscious?

Because Bulldogs are more expensive than most other breeds, they have become a status symbol for some people. Desiring a status symbol, however, is the worst possible reason to own a dog!

Can You Provide Company for Your Dog?

Bulldogs are living, sentient beings who are devoted to their owners. They need plenty of human companionship and pine away without it. They can also become destructive chewers when bored. If you are gone for long hours every day, you may wish to think about a breed that can tolerate longer periods alone. In fact, because Bulldogs are such "mouthy" dogs, they enjoy big, sloppy, wet kisses. If this turns you off, you may hurt his feelings. In fact, the Bulldog's constant demand for attention is frustrating to some busy owners. Bulldog puppies in particular are active and playful, so don't expect him to sleep on the couch all day. This will come later.

Are You a Control Freak?

Bulldogs are not robots. Unlike some "obedience breeds" that stand around waiting for an order, Bulldogs have their own minds. Bulldogs are strategic thinkers, not automatic responders. After all, they were bred to figure out how to attack and bring down a bull! Nobody helped them do it.

Bulldogs are trainable but require exceptional patience. They react extremely poorly to physical correction. Even shouting at your Bulldog can hurt your relationship with him. Young children who spend a lot of time screaming or throwing things can be particularly offensive to a Bulldog. If poorly treated, your Bulldog will never forget it.

The Standard

The breed standard in the United States is similar but not identical to the breed standard in the United Kingdom. Although the American Kennel Club standard has been adapted from the Kennel Club standard, both have been modified a bit over the years.

Due to his unusual physical makeup, your Bulldog should not participate in vigorous, prolonged activities.

Are You an Exercise Nut?

If you are, expect your Bulldog to watch with enthusiasm as you lift weights and run on the treadmill. He won't help and he can't join you. His unusual physique, with its short legs, narrow windpipe, and squashed face, just doesn't accommodate vigorous aerobic activity. (In addition, Bulldogs have tender feet that never seem to toughen up to rough stones or concrete.) Unfortunately, your Bulldog may actually want to join in your games, but he does so at his own peril. He simply can't get enough oxygen to support vigorous physical activity and risks respiratory distress and even death if permitted to overindulge.

Do You Live in (or Can You Create) a Cool Climate?

Bulldogs suffer monstrously from heat and humidity and die more frequently from heatstroke than any other breed. Again, the problem is due to the squashed face and narrow windpipe. Temperatures over 80°F (27°C) can be dangerous to Bulldogs. If you live in South Carolina, for example, you'll have to crank up the air conditioner. And while Bulldogs enjoy the brisk fall weather, bitter cold is not their style, either. They weren't born to pull sleds.

Are You an Apartment Dweller?

Bulldogs thrive in the city as long as the smog doesn't get too bad. They enjoy leisurely walks in the neighborhood meeting everyone, and their equable temper makes them unlikely to panic at the sound of a horn honking. However, apartments with elevators are preferable, as Bulldogs don't appreciate long flights of stairs. They start wheezing, and it's not a pleasant sound. On the other hand, Bulldogs are not big barkers, a great advantage when living in close quarters to neighbors.

Do You Enjoy Swimming?

I hope you like swimming alone, because even though Bulldogs love water, they are really poor swimmers. If they should fall into a pool, they won't be able to get out and will likely drown. If you have a spa, hot tub, or pool, it needs to be fenced off from your Bulldog. However, he will enjoy sitting on the pool steps in the cool water watching you do your laps, as long as someone is there to closely supervise him.

Status Symbol

Even if you yourself aren't interested in any supposed "status value" of Bulldog ownership, others may be. Owning a status symbol like a Bulldog requires vigilance, because they are one of the most frequently stolen breeds.

Can You Handle Snoring?

Bulldogs snore. A lot. Snoring is normal for the Bulldog and is caused by the large amount of soft palate characteristic of the breed. It shouldn't cause you undue worry unless there's an abrupt increase in the noise, which could indicate an airway blockage.

Can You Stand a Lifetime of Cuteness?

Most breeds lose their puppy charms as they mature. Not a Bulldog. That cute mug stays on. And you'll find yourself smiling every time you take a look.

Do You Like Lapdogs?

You do? Good, because your 50-pound (23kg) Bulldog thinks he's a Pekingese. He will demand your lap space.

Do You Have Access to Good Vet Care?

Not all veterinarians can deal with the special problems and needs presented by this breed. Bulldogs are very sensitive to anesthesia and suffer a number of respiratory ailments. Your Bulldog is safest if you have a vet with 24-hour-a-day service.

Are You Willing to Groom Your Bulldog Every Day?

While Bullies don't have a heavy coat, their numerous wrinkles require daily attention. They are also subject to certain skin conditions that make regular grooming beneficial. Regular grooming will reduce shedding as well.

You should brush your Bulldog's teeth every day, especially since he's going to be kissing you all the time.

Do You Have Other Dogs or Pets?

That's fine! While Bulldogs are not pack dogs like Beagles, they don't object to the presence of other dogs or even cats. Of course, Bulldogs require the same socialization any other dog would, but in general, Bulldogs are willing to make friends with the other household pets. They do have a streak of jealousy, however, and some Bulldogs who are not well-socialized can be aggressive toward other dogs.

Do You Want a Watchdog?

Forget the Bulldog. While some bark at the arrival of strangers,

The Bulldog is a great family dog who gets along well with children.

others don't. Some people insist that even though the Bulldog appears to be asleep, he will react very quickly to a suspicious sound. They enjoy meeting new people as well and should not be considered guard or attack dogs. If actually threatened, a Bulldog might take action, but he won't guard your possessions.

Do You Want a Family Dog?

A Bulldog is just perfect for families. While Bulldogs may prefer one member of the family over another, they are not "one-person" dogs and cheerfully adopt everyone as their own.

Do You Have a Sense of Humor?

You'll need one. On the other hand, if you don't have one now, a Bulldog will help you to develop one!

APPEARANCE

The Bulldog is probably one of the world's most unusual-looking dogs. In order to take a closer look at the Bulldog, we'll examine the American Kennel Club and Kennel Club's standards for the breed. (A breed standard is a written picture of the ideal Bulldog.) While no one animal is "perfect," all good Bulldogs should approximate these specifications. Standards are written for show dogs, and it doesn't matter a bit if your Bulldog's tail, ears, color, or feet don't "make the grade." These things don't make him a better pet. However, the

Eye Fact

In actual fact, all dogs have about the same size eyeball — 11 millimeters — no matter how large or small the dog is and no matter how much of the eyeball is visible to the observer.

farther your dog strays from this ideal word picture, the less he is likely to become a conformation champion.

The following description of the Bulldog is based on interpretations of both the American Kennel Club and Kennel Club's breed standards.

General Appearance

The Bulldog is a medium-sized dog with a smooth coat. His body is heavy and thickset, with wide shoulders and sturdy legs. His head is massive and is, for Bulldog fanciers, the most important physical feature of the animal. Even at a glance, the Bulldog should give the impression of stability, strength, and power. He should also have a kind, resolute, and courageous character, as well as an air of great dignity. He should not be vicious or aggressive in any way.

The Kennel Club (United Kingdom) standard notes that the Bulldog is fierce in appearance but possessed of an affectionate nature.

Size, Proportion, and Symmetry

The adult male Bulldog weighs about 50 pounds (23kg), the female about 40 (18kg). The height is usually between 12 and 14 inches (30 and 36cm) at the shoulder. The Bulldog should be well proportioned so that he doesn't appear deformed. Females tend not to have the characteristic Bulldog features to the same grand degree as males, but this is not to be held against them.

Head

The eyes should be round and set low down in the skull, as far from the ears as possible. They should be set in front of the head, like a person's, and wide apart. The eyes should be of moderate size, neither sunken nor bulging. The color should be very dark. The corners of the eyes should be in a straight line at right angles with the stop, which is the place where the muzzle meets the main part of the skull. The eyelids should cover the whites of the eye, and no haw should be visible. (The haw is the red part of the eye you might see in a Bloodhound.)

The Kennel Club standard adds that any dogs showing signs of respiratory distress are highly undesirable.

The ears should be thin and small. They should be set high—as far from the eyes as possible. The front inner edge of each ear should join the outline of the skull at the top back corner of the skull. While various ear shapes occur, the most desirable is the "rose ear." The rose folds inward at the back lower edge, while the upper edges curve outward and backward, actually showing part of the inside. In any case, upright, prick ears, or button ears are not desirable. The Bulldog's ears are never cropped.

The skull should be very big, broad, and square. If you measure the circumference of the skull in front of the ears, it should at least equal the height of the dog at the shoulders. If you look at the head from the front, it should appear very high and very short from the point of the nose to the occiput, the point at the back of the skull. The forehead should be flat and not too prominent; it shouldn't overhang the face.

The cheeks should be well rounded and protrude outward beyond the eyes. The stop should be broad, deep, and very well defined, and there should be a groove between the eyes. There should be an indentation extending up the middle of the forehead, dividing the head vertically right up to the top of the skull. The face should be extremely short, with a short, broad, very upturned muzzle. The nose should be large, broad, and black. Its tip should be as short as possible and set back deeply between the eyes. The distance from the bottom of the stop to the tip of the nose should not be longer than the distance from the tip of the nose to the edge of the underlip. The nostrils should be wide, large, and black, with a well-defined line between them. The lips should be thick, broad, hanging, and deep. In fact, they should overhang the lower jaw at each side. They join the underlip in the front and should cover (or almost cover) the teeth. (In the ideal Bulldog, you shouldn't notice the teeth when his mouth is closed.) The jaw should be massive, broad, square, and undershot. That means it should project out a considerable distance from the upper jaw. It should also turn up. The teeth should be big and strong, with the canine teeth set wide

Chest

While a Bulldog reaches his full height by about four months, his head and chest don't start to catch up until he's about eight to nine months old. These continue to develop until the Bulldog is three or four years of age.

apart and six small teeth located between the canines in a neat, even row.

Neck, Topline, and Body

The neck should be short, thick, and arched at the back. The topline, or line from the shoulders to the base of the tail, should fall slightly behind the shoulders, then rise toward the loins. At that point, the spine should curve more suddenly to the tail. This is called a "wheel back." The body should be well rounded and deep, let down well between the shoulders and forelegs so that the dog appears low and short-legged. The chest should be broad, deep, and full. When observing the dog from the side, you should see a tuck-up in the belly. The back should be short and strong, very wide at the shoulder and narrower at the loins. Unfortunately, the narrow loins of the Bulldog, in combination with the large head, cause the female a good deal of trouble during the birthing process. Nearly all Bulldogs today are born by caesarian section.

The tail can be either straight or "screwed," but it cannot be curved or wavy. It must be short, with a thick root and fine tip, with a downward carriage. If the tail is straight, it should be cylindrical and taper evenly to the tip. If it's a screwed tail, its kinks should be well defined, even knotty. In any case, the tail should rise above the base.

Did You Know?

An undershot jaw is a defect in most breeds, but it is a true hallmark of the Bulldog—it's how he managed to hang onto the bull and breathe at the same time!

According to the breed standard, the Bulldog should have hind legs that are strong, muscular, and longer than the front legs.

While many people have only heard of the American Kennel Club, Kennel Club, and perhaps some other national kennel clubs, an international organization actually exists. The Fédération Cynologique Internationale is the World Canine Organization, which includes 80 members and contract partners (one member per country), each of which issues its own pedigrees and trains its own judges. The founding nations were Germany, Austria, Belgium, France, and the Netherlands. It was first formed in 1911 but later disappeared during World War I. The organization was reconstituted in 1921. Currently, neither the United States nor Canada is a member.

The FCI ensures that its pedigrees and judges are recognized by all FCI members. Every member country conducts international shows as well as working trials; results are sent to the FCI office, where they are input into computers. When a dog has been awarded a certain number of awards, he can receive the title of International Beauty or Working Champion. These titles are confirmed by the FCI. The FCI recognizes 331 dog breeds, and each of them is the "property" of a specific country, ideally the one in which the breed developed. The owner countries of the breeds write the standard of these breeds in cooperation with the Standards and Scientific Commissions of the FCI, and the translation and updating are carried out by the FCI. In addition, via the national canine organization and the FCI, every breeder can ask for international protection of his or her kennel name.

These specifications are somewhat different in the Kennel Club standard, which states that the tail should be set on low, jutting out rather straight and then turning downward.

Forequarters

The shoulders should be heavy and muscular, slanting outward. The Kennel Club standard suggests that the shoulders should look "tacked on" to the body. The front legs should be short, straight, and muscular, set wide apart so that they present a bowed outline. However, the actual bones of the leg should be straight and not bowed. It only looks that way because they're set so wide apart. Nor should the feet be too close together, which would increase the bowed effect. The elbows should be low and stand out loose from the body. The feet should be medium in size but compact. They may be straight or slightly turned out. The compact toes should have high knuckles and short, stubby nails.

Hindquarters

The hind legs should be strong, muscular, and longer than the front legs. This makes the dog higher in the back than in the front.

The wrinkle over the nose is called the "nose rope."

The stifle (the joint between the thigh and "second thigh") should turn out slightly, which causes the hocks to approach each other and the hind feet to turn outward. As with the front feet, the hind feet should be medium in size but compact. The compact toes should have high knuckles and short, stubby nails.

Coat and Skin

The coat should be straight, short, smooth, and flat, with a fine texture and glossy appearance. The skin should be soft and loose, especially around the shoulders. There should be plenty of heavy wrinkles around the head and face. From jaw to chest should hang two loose folds called dewlaps.

Coat Color

Bulldogs fanciers who follow the American Kennel Club standard like pure, brilliant coat colors, and the following colors are listed in order of preference: (1) red brindle; (2) other brindles; (3) solid white; (4) solid red, fawn, or fallow; (5) piebald (large patches of two or more colors). However, a good clear piebald is considered better than a "muddy" brindle. Solid black is not desirable, although it can appear in piebald patches. The best brindles have a fine, even, equal distribution of the composite colors. A small patch of white is allowed on brindles and solid-colored dogs. In piebalds, the color patches should be well defined, symmetrically distributed, and of pure color.

According to the Kennel Club, permitted colors (no order given) include whole ("solid") or smut. ("Smut" means a solid color with a black mask or muzzle.) The only whole colors allowed are brindles; reds with their various shades; fawns, fallows, etc.; white; and pied (i.e., a combination of white with any of the foregoing colors). Dudley (brown),

The Bulldog has a kind, peaceful, and courageous temperament.

The Benefits of Bulldog Ownership

Everyone knows that companion dogs, just by hanging around doing nothing (like your Bulldog), can provide companionship. They also help lower blood pressure and assist people in coping with depression and stress-related disorders. Interestingly, not only does your blood pressure decrease when petting your dog, but his does also. Researchers from the University of Missouri-Columbia found that a few minutes of petting dogs prompts the release of "good" hormones in human beings, including serotonin, prolactin, and oxytocin. These make us more alert, less sensitive to pain, and smarter.

However, there's an additional benefit. When we pet our dogs, levels of stress hormones like cortisol, a hormone that regulates our appetites (especially our craving for carbohydrates), decrease. As a result, you'll find it easier to stay away from the jelly doughnuts!

Petting, of course, is beneficial to your dog as well. It actually has been shown to lower his heart rate and blood pressure. Psychologically, it reassures him and helps cement a loving bond between the two of you.

black, or black with tan are highly undesirable. The acceptable colors should be pure and brilliant.

Gait

The Bulldog moves in a peculiar loose-jointed, shuffling way. It's a kind of sidewise motion that gives a characteristic "roll." Despite this unusual gait, the Bulldog must move in a free, unrestrained, vigorous manner.

The Kennel Club standard reads a bit differently, describing the moving Bulldog's gait as peculiarly heavy and constrained. He should appear to walk with short, quick steps on the tips of his toes, hind feet not lifted high, appearing to skim the ground, and running with one or the other shoulder rather advanced. At the same time, the British standard emphasizes that soundness of movement is of the utmost importance.

Temperament

The Bulldog is kind, peaceful, and courageous. All of these attributes should reveal themselves in his expression and behavior.

CHARACTER AND TEMPERAMENT

Appearance isn't the only factor contributing to the Bulldog's infinite charm. I would like to refer to his personality, but that word

Supervision and guidelines provide the keys to a successful relationship between children and Bulldogs.

is much too weak. The Bulldog has more than personality; he has character—a unique character. He is solid, sensible, and patient. The Bulldog is not a push-button kind of guy who will cater to your every whim, but he'll make a good-faith effort to figure you out—at least to the point where you're waiting on him, rather than vice versa.

The Bulldog is not for everyone. Control freaks who need a push-button dog would do better with a different breed. This is a stubborn dog who ranks low on every "trainability scale" ever devised, although females are probably a little more trainable than males (especially in terms of housetraining) and may respond better to the subtle cues of obedience work. If your previous dog was a retriever or a German Shepherd, you're in for a big shock, but not necessarily an unpleasant one. If you like to take things easy and enjoy the simpler pleasures of life, the Bulldog is for you. Senior citizens, people with physical disabilities, and those who don't feel the need to plunge into the wilderness every weekend connect especially well with the sedate, ultra-civilized Bulldog.

The Bulldog is one of the safest and most reliable dogs around children because of his pretty limitless tolerance and fondness for small ones. This doesn't mean a child should ever be allowed to tease or abuse a Bulldog, of course. Fortunately, Bulldog breeders have done a thorough job of breeding out aggression in a breed whose powerful jaws make an aggressive Bulldog a very dangerous one.

As gentle as they are, however, a Bulldog will not back down from a fight if one is forced upon him, and if necessary he will defend his family to the utmost. This dog does not know fear. In some cases, Bulldogs don't like other dogs, especially when males are involved. If you have other pets, you'll need to socialize your Bulldog carefully.

There are no major differences in the temperament of males and females; individual differences count for much more than gender stereotypes. Different owners will have different experiences with their Bulldogs, regardless of gender.

Your Child and Your Dog

While dogs and kids are born to be friends, common sense tells us that supervision and guidelines are the keys to happiness. Puppies are especially at risk from overexuberant or cruel children. Always remember that you are the parent and you are the dog's owner, so the ultimate responsibility for your Bulldog's welfare is yours. The Bulldog is on your side, however! Bulldogs love children and only need to be given an opportunity to make friends. Some animal experts say that the best time to add a dog to your family is when the children are between seven and nine years old, as toddlers can injure or be injured easily by a puppy. In my opinion, if you are watchful, there's no reason whatsoever why a younger child cannot enjoy the family Bulldog. Besides, recent studies have shown that early childhood exposure to pets reduces the chances of children developing all kinds of allergies, not just allergies to pets!

Along with the joys of puppy ownership, kids can learn responsibility. Picking up dog toys, walking the pup, straightening the bed, riding along to the vet clinic, and helping to prepare the puppy's meals are all ways to teach responsibility and help cement the bond between child and dog. Older children can also participate in training. All children should also be aware of the "five no's" of puppy ownership: no hitting or screaming, no dragging, no table feeding, no pestering, and no hugging (which sometimes turns into unintentional strangling—at least that's how the dog sees it).

Always remember that the adult member of the family is responsible for the Bulldog's well-being. While having a pet is a good way for children to learn responsibility, the pet should not pay the price if the child forgets or becomes bored with the dog. Adults, not children, are ultimately responsible for making sure the dog is fed, walked, vetted, and loved.

The following are some guidelines to help your child and your Bulldog live in harmony.

• Obviously, striking a puppy is cruel and counterproductive. Causing pain to another being is not a good way to induce either love or obedience, only resentment and fear. Bulldogs are bred to have excellent dispositions and are tolerant to pain, but they have tender feelings that can be permanently damaged by violence to their persons. Unfortunately, a Bulldog is so unusual-looking that some children may be frightened by his appearance. You'll have to be quick and proactive here, explaining how your dog is not a danger.

• Dragging a dog along on a leash seems to be a specialty of the uninitiated, including children. Teach your children to use a treat to lure the puppy when he decides he's walked far enough. If the child still can't get him to move, have her ask for adult help. While it's tempting to give the dog those leftover lima beans from your plate, doing so will only encourage the dog to beg for (and then demand) table feeding. Prevent the problem before it starts.

• Children may become so attached to the puppy that they want to be with him all the time. Teach your child that puppies need time to sleep, think, and dream about the universe. When a puppy walks away from a child, he is saying, "Thanks, I've had enough of you for the moment." Continuing to elicit play after a dog has turned his back is asking for trouble.

• Hugging a dog means affection to us. For a dog, it's a dominant, smothering action they may accept from an adult but not from a child. Ask your children to stroke the dog gently on the chest instead.

C h a p t e r

3

PREPARING
for Your Bulldog

I t's relatively easy to make the decision that a Bulldog is just right for you. It's much more difficult to find one. (Never buy a dog as a present for someone else. People need to make their own decisions about this critical matter.)

In the first part of this chapter, I'll suggest several options for finding the perfect Bulldog for you. Later in the chapter, I'll talk about how to get ready for his arrival.

FINDING A BULLDOG

Here is my best advice on finding the right Bulldog for you. No matter what your source, don't get a dog with whom you feel uncomfortable. It's your money and your heart. Speaking of money, you'll discover that Bulldog puppies are pricey. About 90% of Bulldog puppies are born by caesarian section. (In the cases of those who aren't, it's usually an accident.) Obviously, this adds to the cost. Litters are often rather small, too, which raises the price.

Puppies are exceptionally charming, but they are not right for everyone. They need much more supervision, attention, and of course, training, than an adult dog. Because they are an independent breed, Bulldogs can take much longer (and require much more patience) to train than a puppy. In a way, a puppy is a bit of a gamble, while the older dog is a better known commodity. And practically speaking, you'll probably have to wait longer to obtain the perfect puppy.

That being said, there is something special about raising your own Bulldog puppy. A well-bred dog raised correctly has a degree of confidence and sense of self-worth that can be harder to find in an adult dog who has been raised by someone else.

The truth of the matter is that great dogs can be acquired at any age—

including those who have reached their senior years. Your own circumstances and inclinations are your best guides.

Breeders

Breeder Pros and Cons

The best source for a high-quality Bulldog, one whom you might want to show, is a responsible breeder who specializes in Bulldogs. However, the truth is that really good Bulldog breeders don't live on every block (or even in every county), so you'll have to do your research. It's well worth it, though.

One of the great things about breeders is that you often have a chance to observe all of the dogs in the litter with their mother. The sire may not be on the premises, but remember that each parent contributes half of the genes! If the sire is not present, the breeder should have some photos of him, at least, and tell you some reasons

One of the advantages to purchasing a Bulldog from a breeder is that you may be able to observe the mother of the puppies.

why she selected him as the sire for her litter. The puppy may resemble one parent more than another, resemble both equally, or look like neither of them. But he should look like a Bulldog!

The only downside to getting your Bulldog through a responsible breeder (aside from finding one) is the waiting you'll probably have to do for your puppy. Most responsible breeders have long waiting lists, and so they have no need to advertise in the newspaper or telephone book. What's the best way to find one, then? The best way to find a responsible breeder in your area is to contact the secretary of your local Bulldog club, who may be able to direct you to a member who is planning a litter. When talking with the secretary, ask when the next shows are and plan to be there. To find your local Bulldog club, go to the American Kennel Club's website at www.akc.org, or look on the Kennel Club's website at www.the-kennel-club.org.uk.

Selecting a Breeder

You may have to travel to find a good breeder, and you almost certainly will have to wait (often for more than a year), but it's worth it. One place you can try is dog shows. Even if you don't plan to show your dog, a show is a great place to see what a show-quality Bulldog looks like. You may also get a chance to speak to breeders, some of whom may be expecting a litter. The world of dog shows is pretty mysterious, but go anyway. This is especially important if you think you might like to show your dog someday. If you find a Bulldog you think is particularly handsome, ask his handler or breeder if there's an upcoming litter or dogs from related lines. Don't do this right before a class, however, because people tend to be a little tense then. Approach your target after the classes have been judged. I always start with a compliment to the dog in question. Most breeders are happy to talk with serious students of the breed. If you encounter someone who is rude, chalk it up to "bad breeding" and talk to a more amiable person.

Curiously enough, often the best choice of breeder is the so-called hobby breeder. A hobby breeder is no rank amateur but someone who breeds for the love of the breed rather than for financial gain. This type of breeder doesn't depend on selling Bulldogs to make a living (as opposed to a commercial breeder). She probably takes her dogs to shows because she is proud of them and of her role in producing them. This breeder enjoys breeding a

Did You Know?

The word "pet" means something different to a breeder than it may mean to you. For a breeder, the word "pet" means "non-show quality." To you, it probably means the dog you are going to take home and love. Thus, if you are thinking about showing as a hobby, tell the breeder you are looking for a show-quality dog. Don't use the word "pet," even though he will be one.

A breeder's puppies should be healthy, friendly, and active.

litter occasionally and is interested in improving her line of Bulldogs. Selling to the highest bidder isn't important. You won't see dozens and dozens of dogs locked up in a pen in the backyard. A good hobby breeder has made her dogs part of the family, and these pups will easily become part of yours.

After You've Found Your Breeder

Once you find a breeder, expect to be grilled. Bulldog breeders are very particular about the homes their puppies may go to. Their questions may seem intrusive, but breeders are only looking out for the best interests of their puppies. It means they care, and you will benefit from that caring when you bring home your healthy, well-socialized puppy!

You should have some questions for the breeder as well. If you're not planning to show the dog, explain to the breeder that you are looking for a "pet-quality" Bulldog. This doesn't mean there will be anything at all wrong with the puppy. It just means that in the breeder's opinion, the puppy will not achieve a championship in the show ring. Eyes that are too light, a nose that is the wrong color, or a tail at the incorrect angle are just a few unimportant factors that may limit a dog's "show worthiness" but will have no effect whatsoever on his ability to make a great pet.

Although some people are adamant that they want a "pet-quality" or a "show-quality" puppy, the truth is that it is often very hard to tell at a young age how the dog will turn out. Many a promising pup has flunked out in the show ring, while occasionally a dog sold as pet-quality unexpectedly blooms and turns into a show champion, much to the surprise of his confused owners. To my way of thinking, the first concern should be getting a healthy, sweet-dispositioned dog whose ancestors are of good stock. Of course he should look nice, too, but as mentioned earlier, you can't tell too much when a puppy is only eight weeks old. At that stage, they're *all* cute. It's also possible that if a show-quality pup strikes your fancy, the breeder will offer to co-own him with you. In most cases, this means that the breeder makes the arrangements to show

him, while you can still keep him as a pet most of the time. Don't accept this option without carefully reading over the contract and finding out what is expected of you, though.

Questions to Ask the Breeder

A first-rate breeder will be honest about the shortcomings as well as the glories of Bulldogs, as no breed is perfect in every way. A

The temperament of the mother is a good indication of what the puppy will be like.

good breeder can also provide references from previous customers. It's a good idea to call these people and ask questions about the health and temperament of the Bulldog they purchased. A breeder who's unwilling to supply references may have something to hide. A good breeder will also agree to take the dog back at any time if you can no longer keep him. If a breeder doesn't have the type of puppy you are looking for, she should be able to direct you to someone else. Breeders who don't seem to know or like any other breeders raise red flags.

Unfortunately, not everyone who shows dogs is well-informed or even cares about important health and temperament issues. Some people want to raise dogs who look good in the show ring, but they don't seem to care if the dogs they raise suffer orthopedic problems later in life or even die prematurely from inherited disease. Because Bulldogs are subject to certain inherited eye diseases, ask what visual screenings, if any, have been done. Progressive retinal atrophy (PRA), for example, is a screenable health problem. In this disease, the light-sensitive cells in the retina receive an inadequate blood

The BCA Rescue Network

The Bulldog Club of America is very active in its rescue activities, something not all breed clubs can say. They have a rescue network organized into local rescue groups and more than 100 volunteers all over the country. In 2003, these people found homes for over 800 Bulldogs. The Rescue Network also helps raise money for the necessary veterinary care, kenneling, and training of the dogs.

The goals of the BCA Rescue Network include:

- To accept Bulldogs whose owners can no longer keep them and find responsible, stable, loving new homes for them.

- To rehabilitate Bulldogs before placement by providing necessary medical treatment and training to increase the chances of successful placement.

- To help reduce the population of unwanted pets by ensuring that all rescued Bulldogs are spayed/neutered before being placed.

- To place Bulldogs in suitable homes as soon as reasonably possible, so they can start their "new lives" quickly.

- To thoroughly screen applicants before making placement decisions.

- To inform prospective adopters about the rescue program and the requirements for taking care of Bulldogs.

Local BCA Rescue Network groups decide which potential adopters will receive a dog; most try to place dogs reasonably close to their own locations.

supply. Dogs with this condition first lose night vision, then day vision. There is no treatment, and the disease always affects both eyes. However, it develops rather slowly, giving the dog time to become used to the condition. In the United States, the responsible breeder should register her dogs with CERF (Canine Eye Registry Foundation) and have her breeding dogs examined every year. CERF also examines dogs for ectropion and entropion, eyelid disorders that commonly affect Bulldogs.

Reliable rescues are committed to finding safe, forever homes for their dogs.

Another problem in modern dogs is hip dysplasia, a condition in which the thighbone does not fit correctly into the hip socket. This condition is extremely common in Bulldogs. A similar condition of the front limbs, elbow dysplasia, is also common. There is a test available to screen the parent dogs for these problems, but many Bulldog breeders fail to use it, first because anesthesia is required for the test (and Bulldogs are highly sensitive to anesthesia) and also because most Bulldogs fail the test.

One shortcut I have used to sort out good breeders from bad ones is to ask the simple question, "What are the goals of your breeding program?" If the breeder stares at you blankly, you may want to reconsider buying a dog from her. A responsible breeder, however, will not stop talking about it once you broach the topic. Ask the breeder how long she has been breeding dogs. Although every breeder has to begin at some point, inexperienced buyers are best matched with experienced breeders. You should also ask the breeder how often she breeds Bulldogs. Breeders with large numbers of litters over a short period are suspect. Other questions you may want to consider include:

• What organizations does she belong to, and does she participate in conformation or other activities with her dogs?

• Will she show you the puppies' health certificates?

• What are the strengths and weaknesses of her line?

Finally, be sure to inquire about anything in the contract that you do not understand.

Don't let the breeder tell you that she will send you the papers later. You are entitled to them immediately.

Rescues and Shelters

Rescue and Shelter Pros and Cons

Breeders are not your only option for Bulldog acquisition. Believe it or not, hundreds of Bulldogs are lost, abandoned, or given to shelters and rescues every year. The reason is not hard to find. People acquire these wonderful dogs without understanding their special needs. They then decide that the Bulldog is too much trouble or not right for their lifestyle, so the dog joins the ranks of thousands of other dogs and cats in the same boat.

Most rescue Bulldogs are four or five years old, and some have health or behavioral problems that led their owners to surrender them to shelters or rescue organizations. Some have problems with aggression, some aren't suitable for children, and others have housetraining issues. While taking in a rescue dog is tremendously satisfying emotionally, it's only truthful to say that it can be hard work, too. After all, you won't be able to show such an animal; he may have phobias, medical problems, or bad habits. Yet this can also be true of even the most well-bred dog. He may also be a much older dog than you planned on having. And although he will certainly be less expensive than a dog from a reputable breeder, you'll end up spending just as much money on him in short order—more if you decide to take in a dog with special medical needs. So why would you possibly even entertain such an idea in the first place?

One important reason is that adopting a dog from a shelter or rescue makes a real, tangible difference in more lives than you can imagine. First of all, every shelter, every pound, and every rescue group in the country is full. Every day, thousands of dogs are put to sleep, not because they are ill or vicious, but because there is simply no more room for them. Few dogs who go to the shelter will find homes, and every 6.7 seconds a dog is euthanized. Rescue groups have better success, but most are too small to take in large numbers of dogs. When you accept a shelter or rescue dog into your home, you are making room for another dog who may now have a chance at life. You've saved two dogs!

The difference you'll make in your new dog's life is immeasurable. You may be providing your rescue dog's first toy, bed, and love. You may be taking him for his first walk, his first romp, his first visit. You may be giving him the first kind words he's ever heard. However, the biggest difference will be in your own life. The feeling of knowing you saved a life will enrich your own. The love you get from a previously unloved and unwanted dog easily matches any puppy devotion. Bulldogs in particular have loyalty to spare; your new dog will not "pine away" for his former owners, most of whom neglected him. He will transfer his abiding affection to you. Even elderly dogs make excellent pets, usually giving remarkably little trouble. Most of them are happy to live out their last few years in peace, sunning themselves on the porch and going for walks around the block. I have an elderly

The best Bulldog puppy is one who is friendly without being aggressive.

friend who recently adopted a senior female dog, saying happily, "We can be old ladies together."

Selecting a Rescue or Shelter

Some rescues and shelters are responsible and some are not, just as with every other source for finding a Bulldog. Choosing a rescue that is associated with a national Bulldog club is a good option, if you can find one near you. Ask for references or the names of others who have adopted from the rescue.

Just as you would probably have to wait for a Bulldog puppy from a breeder, you may have to wait for a rescue also. This will depend on the availability of the dog, your willingness to travel, and your specific needs. Some people manage to get their rescue dog in just a couple of weeks. Others have waited five years.

A reliable rescue issues a contract the same way a good breeder does. Nearly all rescue groups stipulate that if the dog doesn't suit or can't adapt to your family, you will return him to the rescue, not resell him or give him away. Most rescues also require a home visit and vet check before they will allow you to adopt one of their dogs. The dogs they deal with have already been severely traumatized; rescue groups want to make sure that the new home will be the last one.

Questions to Ask the Rescue or Shelter

Be diligent in asking the rescue or shelter relevant questions about the dog's age, health, and temperament. Find out how the dog ended up in the shelter. If he was given up by his former owner, ask if you can contact this person. Chances are that you won't be able to, but it never hurts to ask.

Bulldog puppies should look clean and healthy.

Becoming a Good Citizen

Good Bulldog owners are first of all good citizens. Don't consider a Bulldog if your lease agreement doesn't allow you to have a pet. Also, don't overstock your house with Bulldogs—many localities permit only a certain number of dogs before you have to apply for a kennel license and subject yourself to special regulations.

If you do have permission to get a dog, comply with all regulations regarding dog licensing and vaccinations, including rabies. Be aware that you are responsible for where your dog poops, and be prepared to pick it up!

Remember, if your Bulldog is off your property, he needs to be on a leash. While he is not likely to go charging off on a trek into the wilderness, he can get into trouble remarkably quickly. Play it safe.

The truth is that no rescue or shelter can give you an iron-clad guarantee about their charges. However, a good shelter or rescue will take the dog back readily if he proves not to be a good fit in your home.

CHOOSING THE RIGHT BULLDOG FOR YOU

Physical Appearance

The eyes and ears of the Bulldog puppy should be clear and free of discharge, and the coat should have a clean, healthy appearance. The gums should be a healthy pink color, not pale or red. The puppy should exude that delicious "puppy scent." Puppies with swollen tummies might have a severe roundworm (*Toxocara canis*) infestation. Nearly all puppies are born with a case of roundworms, but this problem should be resolved by the time you are ready to choose your puppy. Of course, you will make arrangements for the puppy to see your own veterinarian immediately for a general checkup to make sure that everything is in good order. In male puppies, both testicles should be descended into the scrotum. Dogs with only one descended testicle should be avoided. If you can't tell, ask your vet to check for you.

While looking at the litter of puppies, take some time to examine the dam (and sire, if present) also. These animals are the surest indication of what your puppy will look like when he reaches maturity.

If you are adopting or purchasing an adult Bulldog, ask permission to take him to your veterinarian for a thorough physical checkup before you sign the contract. A good rescue will insist you do. Also be sure to ask for all veterinary records.

Temperament

Looks are not the only important thing to consider when selecting a Bulldog puppy. Temperament, including aggression and shyness, is largely inherited, so make sure the dam is friendly, mild, and outgoing, assuming these are qualities you want in your own puppy.

Choose a puppy who is friendly without being aggressive. A shy or retiring puppy may be ill or too reserved to make a good family pet, but a more reserved puppy may be just the choice for a quiet single person. Regardless of your personality, it's very possible that you will find a puppy or dog whose personality perfectly matches yours. Choosing the right puppy ultimately depends more on intuition than on logic. I always feel that when you see the right puppy, you'll just know it.

It's also a good idea to perform a little sociability test with your puppy prospect. He should follow you happily, and when you kneel down and call him, he should toddle over to you eagerly and not fear eye contact. If a puppy seems unduly frightened of a noise that is not terribly loud (pills shaken in a bottle, jangling change), he may not be secure.

The adult Bulldog should have many of these same characteristics. Overall, he should be friendly and confident, with no trace of viciousness or shyness.

The Show Dog

If you're in the market for a show dog, it's important to find a show breeder who will work with you and mentor you. To improve your chances of getting a show quality dog, you may have to settle for an older puppy (five to eight months old) who will give better indications of what he'll be like at maturity than an eight-week-old will. But remember that nothing is guaranteed. Be prepared to love and adore your Bulldog whether or not he turns out to be "show quality." You know he's the most beautiful dog on earth, and that's what counts.

AKC Registration

Even though many people believe that a dog registered with the American Kennel Club must be a high-quality dog, this isn't necessarily the case. The AKC is a registry body only, and so your AKC registration certificate does not guarantee the quality or health of the dog. Some AKC dogs are Westminster champions, while others are poor-quality animals of ruinous health and terrible conformation.

Sometimes a breeder may offer you an older puppy or young adult dog who may not have "worked out" in the show ring. Don't overlook this opportunity for getting a very nice dog at a lower cost. An older Bulldog will bond to your entire family quickly. The same is true, of course, of a rescue dog.

Overall, it's important to spend plenty of time with the litter. You may even want to return in a day or two to look again. A good breeder will not hurry you or pressure you into buying a certain puppy. On the other hand, it's possible that the puppy you have your eye on will be sold out from under you unless you put down a deposit or make special arrangements with the breeder.

PAPERWORK

One bit of paperwork that comes with a purebred Bulldog is a pedigree, which is really just a family tree of your dog. If you live in the United Kingdom, be sure to ask if the dog is being sold on a Bulldog Breed Council Puppy Contract.

In the United States, you will receive the puppy's registration certificate properly filled out by the seller or his application for registration, a copy of the pedigree, and a record of his vaccinations and wormings. All items should be dated and signed. When you complete your portion and submit it with the proper fee, this form will enable you to register the dog, and you'll receive an AKC Registration Certificate. Paperwork should include the following:

For a Dog Not Yet Individually Registered:
- Breed
- Sex, color, and markings
- Date of birth
- Litter number (when available)
- Names and numbers of sire and dam
- Name of breeder
- Date sold or delivered

For a Registered Dog:
- Breed

- Registered name
- Registration number
- Date sold or delivered

You should also receive some written care instructions, including the kind of food the puppy is accustomed to eating and how much and how often. In most cases, the breeder will give you a supply of the food to tide you over until you can buy some yourself. You may also receive a favorite toy or some of the bedding the puppy is used to.

A breeder will also supply a sales contract that includes the terms under which the puppy is sold.

BRINGING YOUR BULLDOG HOME

Now that you've purchased or adopted your dog, it's time to bring him home!

Your new puppy will feel more secure if you allow him to sleep in your bedroom with you.

Timing

Timing your Bulldog acquisition properly is very important. For most people, acquiring a dog during the holidays is a bad idea. With so much going on and so many visitors tramping in and out, a holiday can be a bewildering time for new dogs and new owners. It's usually best to wait until things settle down. However, for some people, holidays are perfect. Teachers, for example, often have time off from classes and thus find themselves with more time to work with a new dog. Still, if it's the dead of winter and you live in a cold place, it might be a good idea to refrain from getting a dog until the spring thaw. Nobody wants to attempt housetraining during a blizzard, including your puppy.

Remember that although this is a thrilling day for you, your new puppy may not be so happy about the experience. From his point of view, he's been dognapped from the only home he's ever known, put in a car where he might have gotten sick, and brought to a new, strange-smelling place with people and possibly other pets he's never seen before. Don't blame him if he's not as overjoyed as you'd like him to be. He misses his mother, littermates, and former family. On the other hand, Bulldogs are good-natured and adaptable. He will quickly bond to your family.

The First Night

If your new Bulldog is a puppy, he'll need plenty of sleep. It's easy for overexcited family members to "overplay" the puppy, but if you remember that he's much like a human baby who needs his beauty rest, you'll have a happier Bulldog.

Both adults and puppies may experience distress at having left their previous home. This is normal. Keep to your dog's former routine as much as possible to lessen the shock, and provide plenty of comfort and support. Schedule and routine is very important. Feed at the same time and place every day. He'll soon regard your home as his own.

Give your Bulldog his own special spot in the house. The spot will be where his crate is set up. If you don't choose to use a crate, you can still have a special spot with the dog's blanket, bed, and toys. This will be his private retreat, the spot to which he can repair when things get rough at home. Never use this space as punishment.

The first night is bound to be traumatic. There's a lot of noise

Wiggly Puppy
Don't allow young children to carry the puppy. Even a careful child can drop a wiggly dog, and your puppy could be seriously injured or frightened. Let them hold the puppy in their arms while they are seated, preferably on the ground.

and confusion, and he's just been put in a strange room and left alone in the dark. Why shouldn't he cry? The solution is so easy. Simply allow your new puppy to sleep in the bedroom with you, in his own bed by your side. There is no need to terrorize him by forcing him to sleep alone in a distant part of the house. Furthermore, it will ease your housetraining chores considerably if you are close to your puppy. When you sense he's beginning to stir, you can jump right up and head outside with him into the bitter cold night.

Having your puppy sleep with you in your bedroom will not "spoil him." It will not make him vicious. It will not turn him into an uncontrollable alpha dog. It will simply make him aware that you are his parent and you will be there to comfort him the way his own mother did before you. Some people allow their dogs to sleep in the bed with them, and if you are entertaining this idea, you can start him right off snuggled by your pillow. This will make your dog more, not less, secure. However, because I strongly advise that you crate train your puppy, it may be best to allow him to sleep by your side in his own crate. That way he won't fall off the bed or wander around the house and get into trouble.

If your puppy cries during the night, talk to him quietly (tell him a few jokes) until he falls asleep. Make sure he is warm. He may wake up a time or two during the night, but this is normal. He'll soon sleep contentedly throughout the night.

Spay and Neuter

Puppies can actually be safely spayed or neutered when they are only a few weeks old, and this is a plan many shelters follow to help curb the pet overpopulation. Some people even think it's better to do it at this age, since young puppies heal so fast. Most veterinarians still prefer to wait a bit longer, however, as they believe the surgery is easier. Some also believe it's better for the puppy to mature before neutering.

SPAYING AND NEUTERING

Unless you are planning to show your puppy, there is no reason not to neuter or spay him or her.

Neutering or spaying offers many advantages:

- Reduces aggressive behavior
- Lessens the tendency to wander
- Eliminates or drastically reduces "marking" in males
- Practically eliminates the possibility of uterine infections and cancers, ovarian cancer, and prostate and testicular cancers.

The procedure is really a very simple one, and terrific new anesthetics let your dog wake up sooner after the surgery, without that "anesthesia hangover." This is important for Bulldogs, many of whom have trouble with anesthesia. Because the surgery doesn't involve cutting into muscle, dogs recover quite quickly (just a day or so), with very little pain. To receive the optimal health results from spaying your female, have it done before the first heat cycle, which occurs at five to six months of age. This will vastly reduce the chances of mammary cancer. If you wait until your dog goes through three to four heat cycles, there is no reduction in cancer risk.

Sturdy, stainless steel food and water dishes are hard to break and easy to clean.

Don't give your dog any food or water the night before the neutering or spaying (he or she might get sick), and give him or her a few days to recover afterward. Your Bulldog will be ready to eat and drink small amounts several hours after coming home from the surgery.

BULLDOG BELONGINGS

Your Bulldog will give you all of the love, loyalty, and laughs a person could ever want—all that you need to do is to provide him with the simple things he needs. The first need, of course, is love. And while I know you love your Bulldog, you have to let him in on the secret! Plenty of attention, hugs, quality time, and just hanging out together will fill the bill very nicely. Bulldogs aren't keen on long-distance love, so you may need to adjust your schedule a bit to humor him.

Food and Water

Canine Nutrition

While I talk about this in detail later, remember that your Bulldog requires a high-quality, nutritionally balanced diet. This includes open access to clean, fresh water. If you need to change his

If you want to give your Bulldog one of those silly spiked collars to make him look tough, go right ahead. It won't hurt him, but it will frighten the neighbors sufficiently!

diet, do so gradually so as not to cause gastrointestinal upset.

Your Bulldog puppy will initially consume puppy food, but when he is about eight months old, you can gradually begin switching to a high-quality adult food. Feed the best food you can find. If it seems expensive, look at it this way: A less expensive dog food is lower in essential nutrients than the better brands. Cheaper food may require you to feed more of it to give the same nutritional value. The result? An overweight dog and a higher feeding bill. More about canine nutrition can be found in Chapter 4.

Feeding Schedules

Puppies must be fed more than once a day because their small stomachs can't hold enough food to meet their growth needs. Until a puppy is four months old, feed him three times a day. After that, a puppy can be fed twice a day. Most puppies require three times as much nutrition (per pound) as do adult dogs. Keep in mind, though, that overfeeding can turn a healthy pup into an obese dog. Fat gained when young is not easily lost. Keep an eye on your dog, and don't let him become overweight.

Feed your puppy in a quiet corner, away from kitchen traffic and other pets if you have them. Still, your puppy should get used to you being near him while he eats, and he should accept you petting him while he has dinner. You do not want to encourage food guarding. Sooner or later, some kid will run up and try to grab something out of his mouth; this is a time when a snap or bite is most likely to occur. Preventive training is the best defense. If your puppy gets used to surrendering whatever he has in his mouth to you, you'll have a safer pet. At the same time, you should counsel the kids not to pester the puppy while he is eating.

Food and Water Dishes

Sturdy stainless steel food and water dishes are your best choices for feeding. They're inexpensive, easy to clean, and unbreakable. (Glass and ceramic bowls can break.) Plastic is the worst choice. It harbors bacteria, gives dogs chin acne, and is infinitely chewable. The food dish should have straight sides and a flat bottom. If you get a bowl holder as well, you won't have to worry about the puppy chasing the bowl all around the kitchen.

Collar

A soft, adjustable collar is best. Both the collar and lead should be of fairly lightweight material.

Choke Collars

The use of choke (slip) collars is not recommended. The incorrect use of these devices can result in a neck injury, especially for a puppy. Some trainers object to the "punishment" aspect of choke collars, maintaining that owners will achieve better, longer lasting results using positive reinforcement techniques and plain old buckle collars. In my opinion, the less force (or correction) you need to train your dog, the easier the training, and the closer the bond between you and your dog will be. I would begin training with a flat buckle collar.

Head Halters

The head halter is very popular with some people, but most dogs really don't like it, and most of them aren't designed for the unusual Bulldog face. I'd stick to something more conventional.

Harnesses

Some people prefer harnesses, especially for puppies. Harnesses are also good for dogs with spinal problems or for sensitive dogs

Supervise your Bulldog while he's wearing a lead to ensure his safety.

who don't like collars and head halters. They are very safe but provide less control than other methods. However, there are some exceptions. One new harness developed by Wayne Hightower has a loop low on the front at the bottom of the chest instead of along the back, which makes walking a breeze. I strongly recommend this harness for Bulldogs.

Leash

You should also have a regular 4- to 6-foot (1 to 2 m) leash made of leather, waxed cotton, or nylon. Chain leashes are noisy, heavy, and unnecessary. They give no warning when they are about to break, and they can develop sharp edges. Good leather leashes are durable and comfortable, especially as they age. Beware of cheap leather leashes, however, which can be rough on your hands. The downside of leather leashes is that they are slow to dry out once they get wet. They are also attractive to dogs' taste buds. Never let your Bulldog take the leash in his mouth. Once he gets a taste for it, you're doomed. (Some owners spray their leather leashes with a bitter apple spray or a similar aversive product to discourage chewing.)

Teach your puppy to accept the lead by leaving a short one on him for a while. Supervise him the entire time so that he doesn't catch the lead on anything or chew it to pieces. He will probably fuss with it a bit at first, but he'll soon get used it. When you do pick up the end, follow him for a while. When you take the lead yourself, call the puppy to you gently; when he toddles up to you, give him a treat and praise him. Very soon he will be happily following you everywhere. At this stage, try not to struggle with

your puppy. If he resists, don't tug the other way, but don't give in either. Lure him to you with a biscuit. He'll soon catch on that it's fun to do what he's asked. Keep puppy lessons short—five minutes a couple of times a day is enough.

A baby gate will prevent your Bulldog from wandering into areas of the house that may contain dangerous items.

Pooper-Scooper

As a good citizen, you'll want to keep your yard and neighborhood clean. The advantage of a pooper-scooper is that it saves your back and keeps your nose distant from the object you are picking up. On the other hand, a pooper-scooper is never around at the right time, and it's silly to carry one on a walk. You can purchase sturdy little baggie pooper-scoopers at any discount retailer, but a plain old sandwich bag works about as well and is much cheaper.

Bed

Your Bulldog needs his own bed in his own special place. Choose a sturdy bed that is resistant to chewing. The bedding can be made of any soft, washable material; the "sheepskin" kind is often favored. However, plain old towels or an unwashed t-shirt that carries your scent will work too. A wicker basket is a bad choice for a puppy bed, as it is so attractive to some puppies that they will begin to devour it. Wicker can break off into sharp fragments that can lodge in or pierce your puppy's esophagus, tummy, or intestines.

There is an allergen-resistant bed that is available, made from "breathable" Cordura nylon, a washable fabric tougher than cotton or fleece that traps dust and other allergy-causing particles.

Crate

A crate is an important housetraining tool and general purpose den for your dog. Even though real wolves only den up to have cubs, domestic dogs appreciate the value of their own place if they are introduced to it carefully. Dogs should be crated when traveling and may need to recuperate after surgery, so it's a good idea to get your dog accustomed to it now. Whatever type of crate you choose, your Bulldog really requires something with good air ventilation. Folding crates such as those made by Nylabone have the added value and convenience of being easy to store away when not in use.

If you're using a crate for housetraining purposes, a large crate may be too big, as it offers extra space in which the Bulldog can eliminate. Many large crates can be sectioned off with removable panels to accommodate him as he grows.

Exercise Pen

The so-called x-pen or puppy pen is a portable wire playpen for your dog. It's great for travel or when you need to confine your dog to a specific area of the house. While you are cooking dinner or cleaning the oven, for example, your puppy can watch you safely. Even more important, you can keep an eye on him. Watch for those telltale squirming signs, and you can use the x-pen as a housetraining tool as well as a containment device.

Doggie Doors

Although not practical for every household, a doggie door opening into a fenced yard makes life easier for everyone involved. The door even acts as a housetraining aid by letting your Bulldog come and go as he likes. They install in most wood or composite doors in minutes. The easiest ones for dogs to use have just a clear, flexible plastic panel, but you can also purchase high-tech models that you can adjust mechanically, which will allow you to prevent the dog from going out or coming in.

Baby Gates

One thing you don't want is your precious puppy wandering all around the house unsupervised. Because you will need to block off certain rooms and the stairway, you should choose a baby gate that's approved by consumer organizations. You can purchase some made especially for dogs. However, if your dog is a major chewer, don't get a wooden gate.

Toys

Proper toys for Bulldogs need to be big—too big to swallow! Remember what a big head your dog has. Small balls, rawhide strips, cow hooves, and similarly-sized treats can be deadly. Because of the Bulldog's unusual bite, he can't chew very efficiently. Bulldogs can choke to death on bones and balls more easily than many other breeds. Refrain from giving your dog battery-powered toys, because they can kill if ingested. If you must use such a toy, supervise your dog constantly. However, avoidance is best.

Select safe toys with parts that won't detach and get swallowed. As far as toy material goes, each one provides a special experience for your Bulldog. Rubber toys give the best jaw and mouth exercise; they're ideal for chewers and dogs who spend a lot of time alone. (Some of these are hollow, so you can hide little treats in there.) These toys are also good for playing games with your dog. Vinyl toys usually contain squeakers that dogs love, but

Provide your Bulldog with safe toys that are too big for him to swallow.

they're not very sturdy for aggressive chewers. Cloth toys are comforting to dogs, partly because they become saturated with the dog's own scent. This is probably the kind of toy that your dog will adopt for his very "own." Rope toys are excellent for tug-of-war games. The flavored kinds are also good for chewing, and the fibers often work to keep teeth and gums in shape. While many dogs enjoy rawhide chips and bones, I don't recommend them as Bulldog toys; they can be too easily swallowed and cause injury. Nylon bones, like Nylabones, help keep teeth clean and healthy. The new flavored varieties are especially appealing to dogs.

Don't overstock your dog's toy supply at first. Overabundance can lead to boredom as surely as insufficiency creates destructiveness. The main purpose of toys, from your point of view at least, is to distract the dog from appealing items like your expensive shoes and wallet. Before the toy gets chewed down to swallowable size, toss it away. A new toy is a lot cheaper than a broken heart.

Cleaning Supplies

Non-ammonia-based cleaners and carpet deodorizers are all handy to have on hand, as are plenty of paper towels.

A nail grinder or pair of nail clippers is an essential grooming tool.

Grooming Supplies

You'll need the following grooming supplies to keep your Bulldog clean and healthy. (See Chapter 5 for more detailed information.)

- Brushes
- Shampoo
- Cotton-tip applicators and cotton balls
- Baby powder
- Mustard squirt bottle (clean and empty, of course) to squirt cleaner into the hard-to-access wrinkles, especially under the nose rope
- Nail clippers or a grinder
- Canine toothbrush and toothpaste
- Grooming table (while not a necessity, it may come in handy)

Luckily, Bulldog puppies don't require a whole lot of grooming until they shed their first coat, but it's a great idea to get them used to the process.

Medical Supplies

The following items, many found right in your medicine cabinet, will be helpful to have on hand. (See Chapter 8 for a complete first-aid kit list.)

- Peroxide
- Antibiotic cream
- Rectal thermometer
- Visine for eye irritation
- Benadryl in case of insect bite or sting
- Petroleum jelly
- Lemon juice
- First-aid booklet for dogs

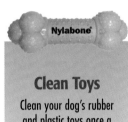

Clean Toys
Clean your dog's rubber and plastic toys once a week in hot, soapy water, and throw soft toys in the washing machine. Dirty, slimy balls and rubber or nylon bones are neither pleasant to behold nor healthy for your dog.

Identification

To protect your new friend, you should make sure he carries ID at all times. No matter what additional kinds of identification you may use, outfit your dog with a flat collar and tag that carries *your* name, address, and telephone number. You can also put the information right on some kinds of collars with a simple laundry marker, so your dog can be identified even if the tags are somehow ripped off.

The latest technology allows you to microchip your Bulldog.

The microchip cannot get lost, nor can it be altered. The microchip is only the size of a grain of rice, encapsulated in a special biocompatible material that allows your dog to wear it safely under his skin. Your veterinarian will implant it between the shoulder blades. (The dog does not have to undergo anesthesia for the process—it is quick and painless.) Once implanted, the microchip is there for good, with no batteries required. These microchips have an estimated lifespan of 25 years and so will undoubtedly outlive your dog. The number of the microchip is entered into a central database, which allows you to notify the company if you move or if the dog's ownership has changed.

If your dog gets lost, veterinarians or humane society personnel have handheld scanners that can be passed over the dog. If a microchip is present, its number will be displayed on the scanner. Of course, not everyone who finds a lost dog has a scanner or knows enough to take the animal to a vet or humane society that does. Therefore, the microchip does not replace traditional ID tags!

Disaster Kit

In addition to your first-aid kit, be prepared for a major disaster, whether it be weather-related or something else. Here's what your dog needs:

- Food (two-week supply—dry food should be placed in airtight containers and rotated every three months)
- Water (two-week supply—rotate every two months; figure that you will need 1 quart of water per day)
- Blanket and towels
- Carrier or crate
- Muzzle or gauze and tape to make one
- Medications, contact information, and vet records
- Food bowls
- Extra collars and leashes with ID on each
- Grooming supplies
- Toys and chewies
- Hot water bottle
- Thick gloves
- Paper towels

- Disinfectant
- Life preserver for dog if you're in a flood area

It is very important to have proof of ownership of your pet in case of a dispute. Make copies of your dog's registration, adoption papers, shelter release, proofs of purchase, and microchip/tattoo or other identification information. Some people have even spray painted their phone number on their dog in case of a widespread disaster. Put the ID information in the evacuation kit as well, along with a list of each of your animals and their species/breed, age, sex, color, and other distinguishing characteristics. Keep current photographs of your animals in the evacuation kit for identification purposes. Include yourself in some of the photos to help establish your claim to your pet.

You should always have a disaster plan for each kind of foreseeable disaster, including a good evacuation place. Keep a list of nearby motels that allow pets. You can even ask if a motel that normally has a no-pet policy will waive that requirement in case of an emergency. A list of boarding facilities may also be an option.

Try as much as possible to take your pet with you—you may not be able to return to claim him. If you can't take your pet, or if he is alone when the disaster hits, prepare by keeping a notice permanently on the front door as to the number of pets inside so that rescuers or kindly neighbors may be able to help remove them. Keep extra leashes and collars in a box on the porch to help get your animals out safely.

PUPPY-PROOFING YOUR HOME

Indoors

Your house is a thrilling montage of dangerous, expensive, and sentimentally irreplaceable items. Your Bulldog will eat, chew, rip up, or urinate on every one of them unless you take proper precautions. Some vets keep files of bizarre items their patients have devoured. I knew a dog who swallowed a 3-foot (1m) necktie (and amazingly passed it). Other swallowed materials have included cell phones, knives, tinsel, dominoes, nails, thermometers, dental radiographs, and a host of other things.

Puppies are drawn to electrical cords, poisonous plants, antifreeze, and human medications. If you have even the slightest doubt, lock it up, barricade it, or watch the puppy like a hawk when he's in the room with it.

What's in a Name?

Although it probably doesn't matter a whole lot what you name your Bulldog, a few simple rules should apply. If you have more than one dog, their names should be different enough that they (and you) can easily tell them apart. The best names are usually simple ones consisting of one or two syllables (although I confess to owning one dog named Tammy Faye Baker-Basset née Russell).

In most ways, your dog doesn't care what you call him, as long as it's not late to dinner. The tone of your voice when you say his name is much more important, and you should only use your dog's name in conjunction with a happy event—not just, "Come here, Otto, so I can give you a bath!" The more pleasant associations a dog has with his name, the more likely he will be to respond to it.

Cupboards

Keep the cupboards locked and put away all household cleaners and medication. (You should never give your dog medications meant for people without approval from your veterinarian, and that includes aspirin.) Use child safety latches for cupboards that your dog can reach.

Garbage

Keep the garbage pail and trash can under the sink or in another inaccessible place. (I keep mine behind the cellar door.) Once dogs start stealing trash, they don't quit, and it's practically impossible to train them out of it. It's much simpler and smarter to manage the problem rather than try vainly to solve it.

Stairways

Close off dangerous stairways. It's bad for a puppy to go bouncing up and down stairs anyway, and you certainly don't want him out of your sight. Excellent baby and pet gates are made for this purpose.

Electrical Cords

Put up loose electrical cords, or at least tape them to the baseboard where they will be less conspicuous.

Houseplants

Many common houseplants are toxic to pets. And even though a grown dog might not be tempted, puppies are oral creatures who test everything in their mouths. Don't leave a puppy unattended, any more than you would a two-year-old child.

Portable Heaters and Fireplaces

Because Bulldogs seek warmth, portable heaters and fireplaces can be lethal for your dog. If you do have a fireplace, use a screen. Put portable heaters out of your Bulldog's reach.

Outdoors

Bulldogs are skillful at getting into

trouble outside the house as well as inside. Some yard items are dangerous, some are valuable, and many are both. To keep your dog and your possessions safe outdoors, fence off areas you don't want him to have access to and pick up toys and trash.

Lawn Chemicals

Keep the use of lawn chemicals to a minimum. No chemicals at all is best, as they are dangerous for dogs. You are walking several feet above the treated area, but your poor Bulldog has his nose right in it.

Fencing

Before you bring your puppy home, check out the fence. Bulldogs are capable of digging under fences as well as shoving themselves through weak spots. If there's an outside gate to your fenced yard, padlock it to keep out dangerous or thoughtless children who think it would be fun to let the dog out.

Doghouse

Many dogs enjoy the comfort of their very own doghouse if they spend time in the yard. Bulldogs appreciate the shady retreat it

offers, as long as they're not expected to spend the night there, or worse, are chained to the thing. Consider the doghouse to be the equivalent of your Bully's outdoor crate that he can wander in and out of as the mood strikes him. However, doghouses can trap heat, so they are poor shelters when it is very hot.

Chaining Your Dog

In desperation from allergies or a passionate devotion to a spotless home, some people resort to chaining their pets outside. This is wrong. It creates a lonely, territorial, barking, sad pet. Chains can entangle your dog so that he injures himself or can't reach food and water.

A dog on a chain is deprived of love, training, and attention. Dogs are social creatures meant to share your life. Very few dogs enjoy spending hours alone. They want to be with you, which is wise of them. They belong there.

Having said that, I will concede that there are times when it's necessary to tether (not chain) your dog. The purpose of the tether is to restrict the dog's movements while you're busy planting petunias or barbequing. On these occasions, you will be outside with the dog and glancing at him from time to time to make sure he is not in trouble.

Seasonal Challenges

Changes in the weather require you to make special adjustments for your Bulldog. This rather unnatural breed can't handle many of the harder blows that nature deals out.

Drafts and Chill

Comfort-loving Bulldogs aren't meant to endure bitter temperature extremities. They aren't Huskies. Their very short noses don't even give them a chance to "warm up" freezing air as they suck it into their lungs, making the cold harder on them than on an otherwise similar, long-nosed breed. Keep your dog dry, warm, and away from drafts. Tile and uncarpeted floors can be cold on Bully tootsies, so make sure he has a warm bed to sleep in.

Walking in Winter's Wonderland

If you can convince your Bulldog to accompany you for a winter's stroll, be sure to wipe the snow and ice off his feet on your return. Many suburban walkways are treated with lime rock salt or calcium chloride, both of which can cause vomiting and diarrhea if your Bulldog licks his feet afterward. (Be sure to clean between his toes, too—it gets icky in there.)

If you are traveling with your dog, plan ahead to ensure that he is comfortable and safe for the duration of the journey.

Dogs can also fall victim to frostbite, just as we can. Their feet, nose, and ears are especially susceptible, and it doesn't take long for them to suffer from exposure. It may not feel that cold to you, but you're bigger (size conserves heat) and more bundled up than your poor Bully. A coat helps keep his central body warm, but it won't do much for his extremities. Frostbitten skin is red or gray, and it may peel off. If your Bulldog does happen to get frostbite, apply warm, moist towels to slowly thaw the affected areas. Call your vet for more advice.

Deep snow makes it difficult for a Bulldog to accomplish some of his necessary *toilette*. You may have to dig out a space for him.

Summer Heat

Summer heat is a terrible enemy of the Bulldog. Very few dogs enjoy the heat (they can perspire only through the pads of their feet and noses), and Bulldogs are even less adept than normal dogs at dealing with it. Some actually suffer from permanent chronic airway obstruction! (This condition can be surgically corrected.) Bulldogs must be observed and supervised carefully when they are outside in the summer. They must have good ventilation, and in hot areas, they should have access to air conditioning when the outside temperature climbs above 80°F (27°C). Their crates should be made of wire mesh for best ventilation. To keep your Bully comfortable, get him used to eating ice chips from the time he's a puppy. And of course, always provide shade.

When taking your Bulldog out for a stroll in the summer months, do so in the morning or evening when it's cooler, and if possible, keep him off hot asphalt and concrete. Bring along a collapsible water bowl.

Cats

Bulldogs are peaceable creatures who generally get along fine with cats. The reverse isn't necessarily true, however. Playful puppies can unnerve cats, who may respond with severe stress symptoms such as inappropriate urination. Give the cat plenty of time and space on his own. (Lock up the pup if you need to, and make sure he responds to your directions to "leave it." For more information on this and other training, refer to Chapter 6.) And remember that a cat who has been declawed has no means of protection.

TRAVELING WITH YOUR BULLDOG

Life is so much more fun if you can take your Bulldog wherever you go. Of course, you will have to obey the rules of common courtesy first. If you're going to stay with friends, ask in advance if your Bulldog is welcome. The same goes for hotels, motels, and campgrounds. Don't just show up without first making sure pets are allowed and finding out what the rules regarding them are. You can find many of these hotels by going to www.dogfriendly.com.

If you are lucky enough to secure a pet-friendly hotel, be considerate of the other guests. Don't allow your dog to mark the furniture, bark his head off, or defecate without you cleaning it up. If you have to leave your Bulldog alone in a hotel room, put a "Do Not Disturb" sign on the door and tell the front desk there is a dog inside. Most hotels require that the animal be crated while in the room, especially if you won't be there.

Always make sure your Bulldog is properly vaccinated for the area in which you are traveling. For example, leptospirosis is common in some areas but nonexistent in others. Check with your vet to make sure your dog is up-to-date on any shots he may need. Take his vet records and recent photos in case he gets lost.

Also, double-check all identification tags. The tags should include a way to reach you or someone who knows where you are. It doesn't do any good to have the person who located your dog

"Animal Card"

What if you have an accident while away from home? To make sure your pets will receive attention while you're in intensive care, carry an "animal card" in your wallet. This card should contain information about each of your pets, including name, species, location, and special care instructions. It should also give contact information for the person you have arranged to take care of your pet. If you haven't made such arrangements, please do. Even if you get hit by a truck, your Bulldog still needs his dinner!

call your home if you aren't going to be there.

It's also a good idea to take a simple first-aid kit with you, including a safe anti-diarrhea medication. Dogs tend to get diarrhea on trips either from the excitement or the strange water. You should also bring along important phone numbers, including that of your veterinarian, the number of the national pet poison control hotline (US: 1-888-4ANI-HELP), and a 24-hour emergency veterinary hospital near where you'll be staying.

Traveling by Car

Most Bulldogs enjoy travel by car, but if your dog is not accustomed to it, take him for some practice runs before the big day. Feed him about one third of what you normally would before starting out to reduce the chances of his getting sick. However, bring some extra food or snacks with you.

Put your Bulldog in a crate or safety harness in the back seat. You don't want him to turn into a football flying through the windshield when you brake for a deer. If traveling by car in the summer months, keep your dog cool by putting icepacks in his crate. Make sure the crate is well-ventilated.

Whenever you take your Bulldog out, think, "Hmm…what if my car breaks down on the road?" Be prepared for that happenstance. Your travel plans should always include bringing along a leash, a supply of drinking water, and a bowl. If you're traveling during the warmer months, bring a cooling vest or towel that can be wetted, a kiddie pool that can be unfolded, 5 gallons of water (for the kiddie pool), and shade netting or a sun shade.

Even if you don't break down, be prepared to stop about once every two hours. And of course, you should never leave your Bulldog in a hot car, not even for a few minutes. Temperatures can soar to 120°F (49°C) in a closed car even with the windows partway open. Temperatures below freezing are also dangerous for your Bulldog. In addition, under no circumstances should you permit your Bulldog to ride with his mug hanging outside the car windows, charming as the sight might be to fellow drivers. First, you might cause an accident. Even worse, debris or other particles can get into your dog's eyes, injuring or infecting them.

Carsickness

While most Bulldogs love to travel, some don't and experience

Did You Know?

The Humane Society of the United States recommends and supplies self-stick door/window signs for emergency workers and emergency contact stickers for the inside of the dwelling that provide information about the pets inside, pet owner, veterinarian, neighbors familiar with the pets, emergency pet caregivers, pet sitters, and so on.

carsickness. In a few instances, carsickness has a physical basis, usually a problem in the inner ear, which can often be safely remedied with an over-the-counter product. Ginger can also be effective. More often, though, the cause of carsickness is psychological. Perhaps the dog associates riding in the car with unpleasantness (like going to the vet). Or perhaps he is frightened of the noise or motion of the car. Sometimes it's hard to figure exactly what came first, the sickness or the fear. Dogs who are anxious may express their anxiety through sickness, and those who get sick in the car may become increasingly anxious about it. Usually (not always), if the dog shows signs of anxiety (slavering, shaking) before even getting into the car, the problem is most likely anxiety-based.

To help your dog overcome fear of the car, take it slow and make the car a happy place. Try feeding him treats inside the car while the car is not running. Do this often enough for the dog to regard the car with approval. If your dog is afraid to even approach the car, you'll just have to give treats closer and closer to the car until he finally overcomes his fear. This may take some time.

After you've done this, repeat the routine with the car running. Go slow, as trying to hurry the desensitization will backfire on you. When you actually start moving, go for very short trips to somewhere nice, even if it's only a block. Get out and walk the dog. Do this every day until the dog starts to really look forward to his daily car rides.

If your dog still retains his fear of the car, you may have to resort to a medical solution. Nonprescription products may help. In a few cases, you may need to get out the big guns and ask the vet for an anti-anxiety medication.

Traveling by Air

Everyone has horror stories about lost or injured pets on a flight, but you can reduce the risk of potential harm by following the law and using common sense. You will generally be required to supply a health certificate (not more than ten days old), which can be obtained from your veterinarian, and a valid rabies certificate before you'll be allowed to fly. Be forewarned: Many airlines will not transport a Bulldog, especially in the summer months, because of breathing issues. This is why it's essential that you check out the airline's policy on pets before you go.

If you can get your Bulldog on a plane, try to book a nonstop, midweek flight. Try to fly during the evening or morning when it will be coolest.

Most airlines are also quite picky about the crate your Bulldog will be flying in. General rules are that the crate must:

- Be big enough to allow the dog to stand (without touching the top of the cage), turn around, and lie down;
- Have handles;
- Have a leak-proof flooring covered with absorbent material;
- Be clearly labeled with your name, home address, home telephone number, and destination contact information, as well as a designation of "Live Animal" with letters at least 1 inch high and arrows indicating the crate's upright position;
- Be ventilated on opposite sides, with exterior rims and knobs so that airflow is not impeded.

Get the crate well in advance so that your dog can get used to it before the big trip. And make sure your dog is flown as "baggage"

Are You Allergic to Your Dog?

Before blaming your dog for your allergy, make sure it really is caused by the dog. Pets get blamed for a lot of allergies they are really not responsible for. Ask your doctor to test you for pet dander specifically before you blame your dog. If you do suffer allergies due to your pet, you're not alone. Fortunately, unless the allergy is severe, you can take steps to keep both your pet and your health.

First, create a special dog-free zone in your home. (The space should include your bedroom.) Just don't allow the dog in there at any time, and keep the door shut. Change your bed linen (including blankets and quilt) on a weekly basis. It's even better if you can use impermeable covers for the pillows and mattress. Even if the dog can't go in there, you'll carry allergen particles on your clothes, and pretty soon, they'll settle down into the mattress.

Buy some HEPA air cleaners and reduce to the bare minimum the number of carpets, curtains, and stuffed furniture in your house. Clean, vacuum, and dust frequently, and use a microfilter bag in the vacuum cleaner.

Bathe your dog frequently—at least once a week. It won't hurt him, and studies show that frequent bathing reduces allergens by over 75 percent.

Finally, consider immunotherapy. Allergy shots will reduce your symptoms, even if they can't eliminate them completely.

Pet Travel Scheme (PETS)

PETS is a system that permits companion animals from certain countries to travel to the UK without undergoing a period of quarantine. This scheme also applies to people in the UK who want to travel with their pets to other European Union countries.

For more information, visit the Department for Environment Food and Rural Affairs' website at www.defra.gov.uk.

(bad as that sounds) rather than as "freight" (which is worse). If he goes as freight, he may be shipped on a different plane. Finally, keep your dog's nails short for the trip; you don't want them getting snagged in the carrier door.

Airline flight regulations with regard to pets change all the time. Contact the air carrier in advance for specific instructions.

Traveling by Bus or Train

Unfortunately, in most states it's illegal for dogs other than service dogs to ride public transport. But check around, you never know.

If You Can't Take Your Dog

It is not always possible or even desirable to take your Bulldog along on every trip you take. In that case, you'll need to have a plan. If you're lucky, you can pop him over to a relative's house, but that's not an option for everyone.

Vet Boarding

One option is to board your pet. Some veterinary clinics also run boarding facilities, which is your best choice if your dog has a medical condition that requires regular medication, or if the dog may have seizures. However, most boarding facilities at vet clinics are rather spartan and don't offer the opportunities for play and interaction that the best boarding kennels do.

Boarding Kennel

If you decide to use a commercial kennel, ask for a tour before you commit yourself—but commit early. Most kennels fill up a month in advance. Check on when you will be able to pick up your dog. Many do not have Sunday pickup. Good kennels:

- Are clean and free of excrement;
- Have both indoor and outdoor runs (preferably with solid partitions between them);
- Allow dogs frequent access to exercise and play;
- Provide appropriate grooming and bathing services;
- Require proof of vaccination, including bordetella;
- Have a vet clinic nearby for emergencies;
- Allow you to bring your dog's own food, bedding, and toys if you desire;
- Are heated and *air-conditioned*, a must for the Bulldog in the summer;
- Love Bulldogs, appreciate their unique qualities, and understand their special needs.

Pet Sitter

Another option is a dog-sitting service. Some services will house-sit as well as pet-sit; others will make arrangements to come in and walk, feed, and play with your dog. If you are thinking of hiring a pet sitter, make sure to meet her first and note how she interacts with your Bulldog. Ask for references, experience, and check her ability to walk, or if necessary, medicate your dog. You may also want to test her knowledge by asking how she might handle certain dog problems, like vomiting or diarrhea. If you like the candidate, make specific arrangements as to when she will be coming to care for your dog and what else she might be able to do (like get the mail). Be sure that your pet sitter gets your contact information and that of your veterinarian.

Always make sure that your Bulldog is properly vaccinated before you travel with him.

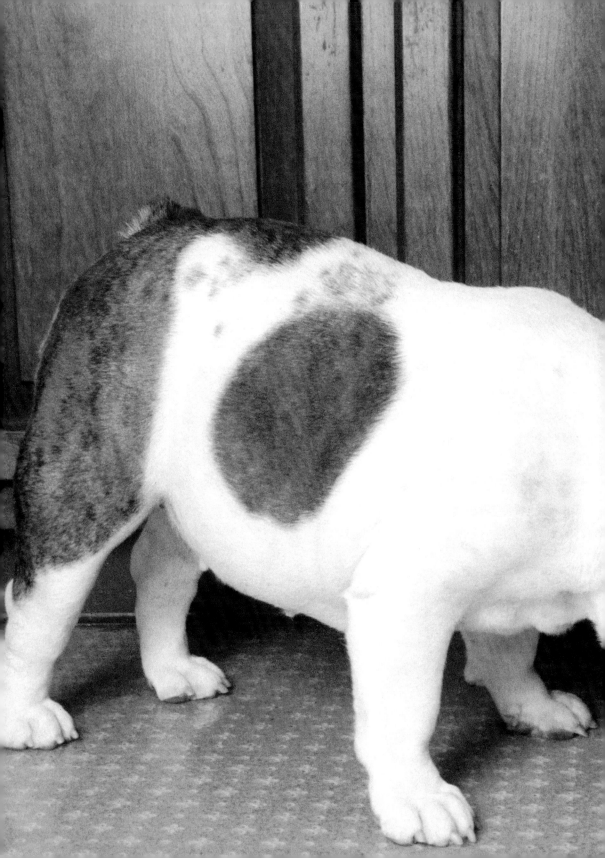

4

FEEDING
Your Bulldog

Y ou may have noticed that your Bulldog eats, well, almost anything! There's a reason for this. Although dogs are technically classed among the meat eaters, they are actually omnivorous creatures. They'll eat anything, from carrots to cockroaches. They'll even eat garbage if you let them. Bulldogs, especially, were not meant to be pampered pets, although that is what they have become. Most of them have an adventurous appetite and will eat whatever they can find. They didn't survive their earliest years by being coddled!

As you probably already know, what your dog eats has a tremendous impact on his well-being. However, to better understand what and how often to feed your Bulldog, it's important to understand how his digestive system works, as well as what nutrients are needed to keep him healthy.

UNDERSTANDING YOUR BULLDOG'S DIGESTIVE SYSTEM

Although we won't be discussing the entire digestive system of your Bulldog, we'll take a quick look down the old alimentary canal.

Nose

It's not a surprise to learn that dogs have much better sniffers than we do. (They don't always smell good, but they smell well.) How well they smell mostly depends on the size of the nose—the bigger the nose, the better the smeller. We humans have about 40 million odor receptors lining the olfactory epithelium membrane; big-nosed dogs may have about 200 million of them. Great nosers like Bloodhounds are good at their jobs because they have big noses in addition to a very determined attitude. I'm afraid your Bulldog will never match big-nosed breeds in this regard, but he's still better at it than we are.

Tongue

The tongue is a complicated, muscular organ that helps your dog take in, chew, and swallow food. Dogs also use it (rather inefficiently) to drink. In order to drink, a dog has to move his tongue around in the water bowl a lot, and he ends up taking in air as well as water, especially when he's a pup and still not very good at it. That's why a puppy will often end up with the hiccups after drinking. Dogs have taste buds on their tongues, too, just as we do, to distinguish flavors. The difference is that they don't have as many. They can also detect sour, sweet, and salt tastes. Their fewer taste buds make dogs more adventuresome in the matter of taste than humans. In other words, they tend to gobble down anything.

Most Bulldogs have adventurous appetites and will eat almost anything.

In the wild, where dogs lived in packs and competed for food, this was a valuable trait, but in today's world, this is a habit that can get dogs into trouble.

Salivary Glands

Dogs have four pairs of salivary glands that produce (what else?) saliva. Saliva is a remarkable substance that lubricates the inside of the mouth, helps food go down easier, and even contains enzymes that start the digestive process.

Jaw Bones

Like all dogs, cats, and humans, the jaws are made of two bones, the upper jaw, or "maxilla," and the lower jaw, or "mandible." The shape of the jaw determines how the teeth are placed. Bulldogs are known as brachycephalic, meaning they have short, wide muzzles.

Teeth

Both sets of jaws are lined with teeth. These include incisors for cutting and nibbling, canines for holding and tearing, premolars for cutting, shearing, and holding, and molars for grinding. Like most mammals, dogs have 28 deciduous, or baby, teeth that fall out and are replaced by 42 permanent teeth. The baby teeth start coming in when the puppy is three or four weeks old; the permanent teeth begin to erupt between the ages of three and four months. Most people can't wait for this to happen, because those little teeth are sharp. In some cases, the baby tooth doesn't fall out when it should. If this happens, misaligned permanent teeth can result. Ask your vet to remove the errant baby tooth.

The tooth has a crown above the gum and a root (or roots) below. The carnassial tooth, that big premolar, has three roots! In the center of the tooth is the pulp, consisting of tissue, blood vessels, and nerves. Surrounding the pulp is the bone-hard dentin that makes up most of the tooth, and capping it all is the enamel, which is even harder than bone (and explains why dogs can eat bones). Around the whole tooth is periodontium, consisting of the alveolar bone, periodontal ligaments, cementum, and gingiva.

Esophagus

Swallowing food takes the meal to its next destination, the esophagus, which is a fairly wide, elastic tube lined with muscles.

Did You Know?

A lot of water passes through both the large and small intestines. The digestive process works much better if the stomach chyme is diluted into a thin slurry. This is one of the reasons why it's important for your dog to get lots of water. The average-sized Bulldog needs 3 quarts of water a day.

The width of the esophagus can be a problem; dogs are able to swallow much larger items than they can comfortably digest. Unfortunately, sharp bones and other bad things can go down the esophagus with ease, only to become jammed in the stomach or small intestine.

Food is squeezed through the esophagus by a process called peristalsis, in which the muscles contract in a wave beginning at the top and ending at the stomach. The esophagus takes a sharp turn when it reaches the stomach to prevent food and stomach acids from being regurgitated back into the mouth.

Stomach: The Mixing Room

The dog's stomach is located within the left side of the abdomen. It contains glands that excrete mucus, hydrochloric acid, and digestive enzymes. The pylorus is a heavy band of muscle that closes the opening of the stomach leading into the intestine.

The stomach's job is to store and mix the food. Because of the dog's historic ability to find and gulp game at one shot, so to speak, the tummy is able to expand tremendously—holding between 1 and 10 quarts (1.1 and 11 liters) of food, water, garbage, or tinfoil, depending on the size, breed, and inclination of the dog.

The stomach is divided into three regions from front to back: the cardiac region, the fundic region, and the pyloric region. The glands of the fundic region add acids and a pepsin-producing enzyme that begin the digestion of protein in the food by breaking down connective and muscle tissue. Moreover, gastric acids help kill bacteria, parasites, and viruses that may have entered the gastrointestinal tract. Pepsin also plays a part in aiding the absorption of calcium, iron, and vitamin B_{12}.

The glands of the pyloric region produce a mucus that protects the stomach wall from the potentially destructive enzymes and acids of the fundic region. The mucus also helps to keep food moist.

Peristaltic waves spread though the stomach, which is sort of like a biological cement mixer. Food mixed with stomach slime is called "chyme." The food stays in the stomach for only three or four hours before moving along the digestive tract. When the chyme reaches the proper degree of sliminess, it slips through the pyloric sphincter to its next station, the small intestine.

Small Intestine: Where It All Gets Broken Down

The small intestine handles most of the tough work of digestion; it takes up almost a quarter of the total gastrointestinal volume of dogs.

The first part of the small intestine is the duodenum, which produces a thick alkaline excretion that neutralizes the acid food from the tummy. The pancreas also ships in some digestive enzymes to help break down the food.

The intestinal lining is covered with small projections called villi. These projections, which are loaded with tiny microvilli, greatly increase the surface area of the small intestine. As a matter of fact, the villi of a medium-sized dog provide an absorptive surface the size of a good-sized bathroom. From the small intestines, nutrients pass into the bloodstream and lymph system. The small intestine also handles the transport of carbohydrates and proteins.

It takes about 36 hours for the digestive process to be complete, but moist food moves a lot faster than dry food.

Large Intestine: Solid Waste Removal

The dog's large intestine or colon has a large diameter, although it's shorter than the small intestine. In form, it's a simple tube that is shaped like a question mark. (There is a cecum, too, often described as part of the large intestine, but this appendix-like pouch is really off to the side at the juncture between the small and large intestines.)

The most important function of the large intestine is to dry out the waste material it receives from the small intestine, thereby conserving a great deal of water. Dogs would need to drink a lot more water if they didn't have a large intestine.

Rectum and Anus

Everything, of course, exits through the anus. The anal region comprises the anal canal and its associated structures. There are many glands associated with the anal region: the circum-anal glands, the anal glands proper, and the numerous microscopic glands located within the walls of the anal sacs. Sometimes these glands are called "scent" glands.

NUTRIENTS, VITAMINS, AND MINERALS

Now that you've seen how your dog's digestive system works, it's time to take a look at what goes into it—those all-important nutrients, vitamins, and minerals that make up your Bulldog's food.

Nutrients

Protein

About 50 percent of every cell in your dog's body is made of protein. Proteins are also critical for building enzymes, hormones, hemoglobin, and antibodies. All animals need protein for maintenance and healing, and young animals need it for growth. If a puppy doesn't get enough protein, his tissues and organs won't develop properly. Proteins are made up of important amino acids that animals need to grow and remain healthy. Dogs need more protein than people do; although no optimum level has been established, even 30 percent of the total calories in a dog's diet is not too much. Protein can be found in many foods, including meat, fish, eggs, and soybeans. However, all proteins are definitely not equal. Not all proteins are digestible proteins, and some are more digestible than others. Digestible proteins are those that can actually be absorbed through the gut wall into the body. This digestibility factor is what is really important, not the total amount of protein. For example, although they are actually omnivores, dogs cannot use proteins derived from plants very well; they need high-quality animal-based protein to do their best.

The digestibility factor of some cereals commonly found in dog food is only about 50 percent. Dogs function best on meat- or fish-derived protein; vegetable-derived protein can cause diarrhea and is incomplete, meaning that it doesn't have enough of all of the different kinds of amino acids your dog needs. Ideally, a dog's diet should be about 75 percent meat, and the rest should be vegetables.

Unfortunately, although the dog food label lists the amount of protein in a food, it doesn't say where the protein comes from. Some kinds of protein are much more usable than others. Hair, for

The proper balance of vitamins and minerals is essential to maintaining your Bulldog's health.

example, is almost entirely made of protein, but try living on a hair diet and see what happens to you!

If your dog doesn't get enough protein in his diet, he may show poor growth, a dull coat, and muscular wasting. (Only protein builds muscles.) Excess protein is usually excreted from the body, except in cases where the dog has kidney or liver damage.

Fat

Fats have twice the number of calories per gram as do protein or carbohydrates; they are packed with energy. Fats keep cells in good working order while adding texture to food and increasing its palatability. Dogs digest fats *very* efficiently and need a higher proportion of fat in their diets than we do to keep healthy. It's particularly important for dogs who have difficulty maintaining weight or who are picky eaters. (Fats contribute immensely to the palatability of foods, which is why cheesecake tastes better than parsnips.)

Dogs can use both plant and animal fats with equal ease. However, oils derived from plants provide large amounts of essential fatty acids (EFAs). These acids are needed for many biological functions. In the wild, dogs eat portions of the vegetable matter contained in their prey's stomach. This presumably supplies them with some EFAs.

Most commercial dry dog foods contain between 5 and 10 percent fat, sufficient for sedentary dogs. Fat also makes food taste better, which is why most dogs prefer any canned meat to dry kibble. Fats also deliver the fat-soluble vitamins A, D, E, and K and help make a healthy coat. Too much fat, however, especially when given all at once, results in pancreatic problems. And of course, it makes dogs gain weight. Insufficient fat makes for a dry coat and poor growth.

Dogs who do lots of work for long periods in the cold, like Huskies running a race, need more fat than the average Bulldog. Good commercial foods are properly supplied with the right amount of fat to fulfill a dog's needs throughout his various life stages.

Carbohydrates

Sugar, starches, and dietary fiber are all carbohydrates. They provide very efficient energy and serve as building blocks for other

Protein Power

Signs that your Bulldog is not getting enough protein:

- Poor growth
- Dull coat
- Muscular wasting

biological components. They are also a heat source for the body when they are metabolized for energy. They can be stored as glycogen or converted to fat. They also help regulate protein and fat metabolism.

Dietary fibers help move food through the intestinal tract and provide bulk, helping an animal feel full without extra calories.

Scientists are still trying to figure out the precise place of carbohydrates in a dog's diet. Dogs can use them to make energy, but are they actually needed? Test results suggest that they may be, at least for pregnant and nursing dogs. It's not a major issue, since nearly every dog food and dog biscuit in the country is loaded with carbohydrates. Excess carbohydrates are stored as fat and can lead to obesity.

Equally important as what nutrients your dog needs is the proportion in which he gets them. This is partly dependent on his individual needs, health, and life stage. Growing puppies, healthy adults, and elderly dogs need different amounts of protein and nutrients.

Vitamins

According to *Stedman's Medical Dictionary*, a vitamin is "one of a group of organic substances, present in minute amounts in natural foodstuffs, which are essential to normal metabolism." Vitamins are naturally present only in tiny amounts, but they are essential for life.

Dogs and people both need vitamins for thousands of chemical reactions that take place in the body. Along with minerals and enzymes, vitamins help with digestion, reproduction, blood clotting, and the normal development of muscle, bone, skin, and hair. Vitamins are also important in the way the body uses protein, carbohydrates, and fats.

Vitamins come in two major varieties, fat soluble and water soluble. Fat-soluble vitamins can be stored by the body, but water-soluble vitamins are excreted quickly and should be supplied every day in the diet.

Because vitamins are present in very small quantities in most foods, many people decide to supplement. This can't hurt with water-soluble vitamins, which are only found within the body in tiny amounts. Fat-soluble vitamins, on the other hand, are usually stored in special fat storage cells called lipocytes. They can build up within the body and may cause trouble if oversupplemented. People worry about toxicities associated with large amounts of fat-soluble vitamins, especially A and D. This won't happen with a regular diet, but it is possible to overdose your dog with them if you supplement carelessly. Always consult your veterinarian before supplementing these vitamins.

Vitamin A (fat soluble)

Vitamin A and beta-carotene seem to enhance immune functions and may help to prevent some kinds of cancer. Be careful not to oversupplement, however. Large amounts of vitamin A are poisonous. A couple of carrots a day will do perfectly.

Vitamin D (fat soluble)

Vitamin D is really a group of compounds that help regulate calcium and phosphorus in the body. It's not known whether dogs need vitamin D added to their diet, since their skin can activate it from the sun's ultraviolet rays. Vitamin D can be found in fish oils, egg yolks, and many meat and milk products. However, if your Bulldog spends much time outside, he probably gets lots of it anyway. Insufficient amounts of vitamin D can cause rickets and other bone problems. Too much can cause hardening of soft tissues, diarrhea, and weight loss.

Vitamin E (tocopherols) (fat soluble)

Vitamin E is a potent antioxidant that helps prevent the oxidation of the unsaturated fatty acids found in cell membranes. Vitamin E helps produce prostaglandins, which regulate blood pressure, muscle contraction, and reproductive functions. In fact, vitamin E may be a good supplement for neutered pets. One form is used in the pet food industry as a preservative. As a preservative in pet food, vitamin E operates much as it does in tissues, preventing the oxidation of the fats that makes the food "go bad."

Vitamin E is found in polyunsaturated vegetable oils like wheat germ oil, corn oil, and sunflower oil. The best vegetable source is probably safflower oil, which contains the very active alpha tocopherol form of vitamin E. Whole grain cereals, cod liver oil, and egg yolk also contain vitamin E. Deficiencies in vitamin E can weaken the immune system. There seem to be no known toxicities with too much.

Did You Know?

Many people are uncertain whether their dogs are getting enough vitamins and minerals in their diets. While this is a legitimate concern, it's easy to go overboard the other way. Puppies are particularly vulnerable to the dangers of oversupplementation. Don't add minerals or vitamins to your puppy's diet without a recommendation from your veterinarian.

Vitamin K (quinones) (fat soluble)

Vitamin K was the last vitamin to be discovered. Dogs generally don't need vitamin K added to their diet; they can make enough of the vitamin from the bacterial synthesis in their intestines. However, when the animal is on a course of antibiotics (which can destroy one form of vitamin K), it is sometimes wise to supplement by feeding vegetables like spinach or kale, which produce vitamin K. Antibiotics kill off some of the normal intestinal bacteria necessary for vitamin K_2 synthesis. Vitamin K helps blood clot as well.

Vitamin C (water soluble)

One of the most interesting of the vitamins is vitamin C. Vitamin C comes in two forms: dehydroascorbic acid and ascorbic acid. Ascorbic acid mixes easily with water and is readily absorbed through the intestinal wall. It also enters the urine. Very little is stored within the body. Dogs can manufacture their own ascorbic acid from glucose, although humans cannot.

While some people think vitamin C cures hip dysplasia, it does not. Hip dysplasia is a genetic abnormality, and not even vitamin C can change genetic structure. Some studies seem to indicate that large doses of vitamin C do result in lessened joint pain, although it can't treat the underlying condition itself.

It's probably helpful to supplement your dog's diet with vitamin C, especially in fast-growing puppies, pregnant bitches, lactating mother dogs, and working dogs. This is a safe, nontoxic vitamin. However, there is controversy raging over the function of vitamin C in the canine diet. Unlike human beings, dogs can manufacture vitamin C themselves, so conventional wisdom tells us that dogs don't need it added to their food. Some nutritionists claim it can actually be dangerous to the kidneys. Other experts, however, tout the value of vitamin C. For one thing, although dogs can make their own vitamin C, they seem less efficient at doing so than all of the other mammals who can manufacture their own. However, dogs who receive large supplements of vitamin C may lose the ability to produce it for themselves. Because vitamin C has antihistamine properties, some theorists believe it helps protect against certain canine allergies. Others think it plays a role in fighting arthritis, along with vitamin E and the mineral selenium. Vitamin C may even fight cancer, both by preventing the occurrence of the disease and as a dietary supplement for cancer patients.

Don't supplement your Bulldog's diet without speaking to your vet.

Thiamin (water soluble)

Thiamin, or vitamin B_1, converts glucose to energy and is needed for the normal function of muscles and nerves. A deficiency of thiamin results in loss of appetite, weakness, loss of reflexes, loss of nerve control, and death. It's pretty rare to have a thiamin deficiency; it usually occurs in animals who have been fed only raw fish, especially catfish, smelt, or herring, all of which contain an enzyme called thiaminase that destroys thiamin. If your dog is living only on raw fish, stop right now.

Riboflavin (water soluble)

Riboflavin (vitamin B_2) is important for growth, muscle development, and maintaining a healthy coat. It is found in organ meats and dairy products. A deficiency of riboflavin causes poor growth, eye abnormalities, rear leg weakness, and heart failure. Such animals may also have fainting episodes, termed "collapsing syndrome."

Pyridoxine (water soluble)

Pyridoxine (vitamin B_6) helps the body use amino acids. It is found in many foods but is destroyed by processing. Pyridoxine deficiency results in anemia, poor growth, kidney stones, tooth cavities, skin lesions, and even death. Pyridoxine is found in meats (especially organ meat), whole grains, and vegetables.

Biotin (water soluble)

Biotin helps maintain healthy skin and hair and is important for growth, digestion, and muscle function. Your Bulldog produces about half the biotin he needs from his own intestines; the rest comes from meat, milk, eggs, and legumes.

Minerals

A dietary mineral is any inorganic component of a food. Like vitamins, minerals are substances necessary for an animal's health. Dietary minerals are generally classed into two main groups: macrominerals (sulfur, calcium, phosphorus, magnesium, and the electrolytes sodium, potassium, and chloride) which are consumed in gram quantities per day, and trace minerals like iron, zinc, copper, iodine, and selenium, needed in milligrams or micrograms per day. A third class includes the ultratrace minerals that have been shown to be necessary in laboratory animals but not in dogs.

Minerals participate in nearly every function of the body. They build teeth and bone, serve as parts of enzymes, and are a vital component of the blood and other body fluids. Minerals also play a role in muscle contraction, nerve impulse transmission, and cell membrane permeability.

Calcium (Ca)

Calcium, composing about 2 percent of body weight, is the most abundant mineral in your dog's body. Calcium is the major inorganic component of bone. In fact, about 99 percent of the body's calcium is found in the skeleton. Calcium is plentiful in dairy products and legumes. Foods high in calcium include bones, eggshell, and leafy green vegetables. In dog food, high levels of calcium are found in poultry by-product meal, lamb meal, and fish meal. This is mostly because of their bone content. Meat without bone is a very poor source of calcium. And milk, while high in calcium, has very little magnesium, which is necessary to metabolize the calcium.

Calcium forms and strengthens bones and teeth, helps in blood clotting, and aids metabolism. A calcium deficiency results in slower, incomplete growth and poor bone and muscle. However, too much calcium, especially when not balanced with phosphorus, can lead to skeletal deformities and joint breakdown.

Phosphorus (P)

After calcium, phosphorus is the most plentiful component of bones and teeth. Phosphorus

Minerals

Minerals are essential for nearly every function of the body. They:

- Build teeth and bones
- Serve as parts of enzymes
- Are a vital component of the blood
- Play a role in muscle contraction

Dietary minerals play an important role in building teeth and bone.

is also involved in most of the chemical reactions in the body. It aids growth and is necessary for muscle contraction. Protein-rich foods also contain phosphorus in abundance. Meat, legumes, oilseeds, and dairy products are rich sources. When phosphorus is incorrectly balanced with calcium, dogs can develop loose teeth and constipation.

Magnesium (Mg)

Magnesium is interdependent with calcium and phosphorus for bone development. Just as calcium stimulates muscles, magnesium helps them relax. Magnesium is found in bones and bone meal, oilseed and protein supplements, legumes, dairy products, and unrefined grain and fiber. Dogs whose diet is low in magnesium could suffer from poor appetite and irritability, as well as muscle weakness.

Manganese (Mn)

Manganese is a component of many cell enzymes, particularly those involved with the production of energy. Sources include cereals and menhaden fish oil. Deficiency is rare. Manganese is a relatively nontoxic mineral, even in large amounts.

Copper (Cu)

Copper is a component of many enzymes that catalyze reactions involving oxygen. Copper is linked to zinc, and its metabolism is

Like calcium, phosphorus is an integral component of healthy bones and teeth.

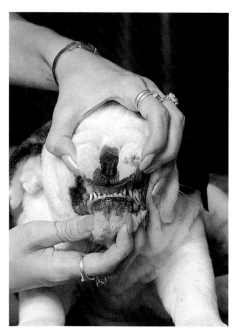

related to that of iron. In fact, copper is necessary for the absorption and transport of iron. It is essential for all cells and enables the incorporation of iron into hemoglobin. It is found in meat, especially organ meat, and bones. A deficiency is rare, found most often in diets lacking sufficient meat intake.

Sodium (Na) and Chloride or Chlorine (Cl)

Sodium and chloride are called electrolytes. Both sodium and chloride help to regulate the acid-base balance and maintain the balance of dissolved substances inside and outside the cells (called the osmotic pressure). Sodium is needed for the absorption of sugars and amino acids in the small intestine. Sodium, together with potassium, is necessary for the transmission of nerve impulses. Chloride forms hydrochloric acid in the stomach.

Sodium and chloride are found in salt and cereals, fish, eggs, dried whey, and poultry by-product meal. A deficiency (very rare) causes excess urination, salt hunger, pica, and weight loss. Obese dogs, hypertensive dogs, and dogs with kidney disease or certain endocrine conditions should probably lay off the salt. Most commercial foods are loaded with the stuff.

Iron (Fe)

Iron is present in every cell of the body, but its greatest concentration is in the proteins hemoglobin and myoglobin. Hemoglobin is found in the red blood cells and transports oxygen from the lungs to the tissues. The best source of iron for dogs is from meat, especially organ meat like liver, spleen, and lungs. It is rare to see a dog with an iron deficiency unless he has been on a vegetarian diet. Except in extreme cases, do not supplement iron. If you're giving your dog a vitamin/mineral supplement, choose one without iron. Since meat and dairy products abound in iron, normal dogs don't need an iron supplement. Iron can be toxic in large concentrations.

Selenium (Se)

Dogs need less selenium than any other commonly recognized trace mineral. It is also toxic in very small amounts. However, selenium helps protect cell membranes from oxidative damage, much like vitamin E. Vitamin E can replace the requirement for selenium in the body, but selenium cannot substitute for vitamin E. Selenium does not cross the blood brain barrier like vitamin E. Selenium is found in eggs, liver, and cereals. However, selenium in fish is not very bioavailable.

Iodine (I)

Iodine makes up part of the thyroid hormones thyroxine (T4) and triiodothyronine (T3), which regulate the metabolic rates of the body. The iodine your dog consumes ends up mostly in his thyroid gland. Iodine is found in milk, fish, eggs, poultry, and iodized salt. Iodine deficiency is rare, found mostly in dogs who receive a diet composed solely of meat.

Zinc

Zinc is an essential mineral that is added to today's commercial diets. However, some puppies, pregnant bitches, performance dogs, or pets with skin problems may require a supplement. It also improves the hair coat. This is because zinc is not well absorbed by the body. Further, plants and fibers contain substances that bind zinc, so dogs fed a mostly vegetable-based diet may develop a zinc deficiency. Too much calcium in the diet can also bind zinc. Dogs with inflammatory bowel disease may develop zinc deficiency. You can find a zinc supplement in good vitamin supplements and in many fatty acid supplements. Zinc is especially important, as it is needed for normal metabolism. A diet deficient in zinc will result in thin hair and crusty dermatitis.

Now that you have a basic understanding of what nutrients, vitamins, and minerals your dog needs to remain healthy, it's crucial that you learn how to interpret dog food labels to determine what foods are best for your Bulldog.

Read the label before you feed your Bulldog any commercial food.

DOG FOOD LABELS ▬

While understanding a dog food label is not more difficult than classical Greek, it is not much easier, either. Still, the careful consumer can figure out at least some of it. It may come as a surprise to learn that as far as federal regulations go, very little is actually required of pet food manufacturers. Companies are required to accurately identify the product, provide the net quantity, give their address, and correctly list ingredients. Pet food companies are not subject to quality control laws. They are also not required by the feds to list the ingredients in any particular order, although some states may require them to do so. In the United States, a little security is found by looking for the AAFCO label.

AAFCO stands for Association of American Feed Control Officials. This organization describes what model regulations pet foods must follow in order to carry the AAFCO label.

AAFCO-labeled foods provide a guaranteed analysis of the food, calorie statement, and a nutritional adequacy statement. This doesn't necessarily mean that the product is good. It means that it's properly labeled. Critics claim that the testing AAFCO performs is not particularly stringent, and it is in no way tantamount to a controlled scientific study. However, the good news is that the highly competitive dog food market is driving up the overall quality of commercial foods.

Today, owners have more good choices than ever before; however, they also need to educate themselves to know what they're buying. When examining a label, start with the nutritional adequacy statement. This tells you what life stage (growth, pregnancy, lactation, and/or adult) the food is intended for. It will also tell you how the pet food manufacturer verified the food's adequacy for the life stage or stages. For instance, the label will probably say that the food was tested either by feeding trials (that's best) or by chemical analysis (not as good). AAFCO sets the guidelines for feeding trials. When a food has been tested through feeding trials, you can be sure that at least some dogs have eaten the stuff for six months without dying or getting sick. This isn't much, but it's something. However, not all dog foods are so tested. Those using chemical analysis attempt to show that the food contains the same basic chemical composition as foods that have actually been tested. This method is a money saver for the company.

The feeding trial is somewhat of a higher standard than chemical analysis, but neither one tells you much about the actual quality of the food. For example, the feeding trial is simply this:

- Eight dogs older than one year of age must start the test.
- At the start, all dogs must be of normal weight and health.
- A simple four-panel blood test (not a complete blood chemistry) is to be taken from each dog at the start and finish of the test.
- For six months, the dogs must only eat the food being tested.
- The dogs finishing the test must not lose more than 15 percent of their body weight.
- During the test, none of the dogs are to die or be removed due to nutritional causes.
- Six of the eight dogs starting must finish the test.

That's all there is to it. This test doesn't take into consideration the differences among breeds or many other important factors. It's not multigenerational either. So while an AAFCO-approved food won't kill your dog, there's no guarantee he'll thrive on it either.

"Meat" Labels

If an AAFCO-labeled product has the word "beef" for its simple

The Calcium/Phosphorus Ratio

Ideally, the calcium/phosphorus ratio should range between 1:1 and 2:1, with 1.1:1 or 1.2:1 being ideal. A diet that is loaded with meats high in phosphorus and low in calcium, or a plant-based diet high in phytates with a calcium content greater than 2.5 percent (DM), can lead to trouble. However, if your dog is receiving the correct amounts of calcium and phosphorus, the ratio takes care of itself. The ratio is more important for puppies, especially large-breed puppies, than for adult dogs.

name, it must be 95- percent beef, exclusive of water needed for processing. Even counting the water, it must be 70 percent beef. These products have simple names, like "Jean's Beef Food for Dogs." The same goes for chicken, fish, or lamb. These foods are all canned; no kibble is 95 percent meat.

"Dinner" Labels

If the word "dinner" or a similar word like "platter" or "entree" is used, each featured ingredient must compose between 25 and 94 percent of the total ingredients. Therefore, "Diane's Sawdust Dinner for Dogs" must contain at least 25 percent sawdust (or whatever the named ingredient is).

"With" Labels

If the word "with" is used, the named ingredient must be at least 3 percent of the total. Thus, "Diane's Sawdust Dinner for Dogs With Liver" must contain 3 percent liver. "Diane's Sawdust Dinner for Dogs With Octopus and Sirloin" must contain 3 percent octopus and 3 percent sirloin, as well as at least 25 percent sawdust.

"Flavor" Labels

If the label reads "beef flavor," rather than "beef," it need only contain enough beef to be taste-detectable. The word "flavor" must appear in letters as large as those of the named ingredient.

TYPES OF FOOD

Your choice of what to feed your dog is practically unlimited: dry food, canned food, semi-moist, "people food," or any mixture thereof. I am not going to tell you that only one kind is right for you and your dog. Many factors come into play: convenience, expense, nutritional value, taste, availability, allergies, and other things. What's right for one dog is not right for all. One rule I do apply is, "Don't feed your Bulldog something he dislikes." Yes, he will eat almost anything if he gets hungry enough, rather than starve. So would I, but that doesn't mean I'd like it. Mealtimes should be pleasurable for everyone, so why not shop around until you find something nutritious that your dog really enjoys? If he seems to like something for a while, then gets bored with it, change his food. It's not difficult.

Whatever you choose, go for quality. The difference between the

Did You Know?

Avoid feeding your Bulldog high-fat dairy products, processed meat, candy, and chocolate. Chocolate is toxic to dogs, while high-fat foods can lead to pancreatitis and obesity. Very salty products, like processed meats and sugary foods like candy are not natural to a dog's diet (or even to ours).

best and worst is just a few dollars a bag, but the difference in nutrition can add healthy years to your dog's life.

Commercial Foods

We have only been feeding our dogs processed food, at least on a large scale, for about 60 years. (The military played a role in its popularization, because the army needed a convenient, easy way to store food for its war dogs.) Nowadays, about 95 percent of American dog owners feed their dogs primarily or solely a commercial diet, usually dry kibble. While most of these products contain the minimum amounts of nutrients to be considered "nutritionally complete," none of them are really an ideal food for your dog. Their greatest advantage is that they are convenient.

Some premium products do approximate top nutrition, but these products can be hard to locate, and you probably won't find them just anywhere. This doesn't mean you can't get them. Look on different companies' websites to find your nearest distributor, or have the dog food delivered right to your door.

When selecting the best commercial food for your Bulldog, remember that almost any kind of meat can end up in dog food. In many places, pet food manufacturers are free to use road kill, cows who have perished from disease, or any other source of protein that suits them. Some companies, however, use only human-grade meat. Formerly, companies were not permitted to state this valuable fact on their labels, a regulation obviously not designed to protect the consumer but designed to protect the farmer, who now had an outlet for his diseased and downed cattle. Fortunately, this regulation has now thankfully been relaxed, so you can easily choose human-grade meats for your dog.

You can avoid the worst food by sticking to some simple guidelines.

1. Avoid dog foods containing "by-products." Meat by-products are those parts of the animal not deemed fit for human consumption. While some by-products are both healthy and tasty to dogs, many more are not. Avoid them.

Many Bulldogs prefer larger kibble, and some research has suggested that dry food, like kibble, helps reduce tartar buildup on teeth.

2. Avoid food laden with grain or cereal by-products. These ingredients are the part of the plant left over after the milling process. They are technically called "fragments," but they appear in many guises on the label. The carbohydrates in food should be whole grains. Many dogs are allergic to soy, so stay away from it.

3. Good food should not contain sweeteners, artificial flavors, colors, or preservatives. The best dog foods are preserved naturally with vitamin E (tocopherols) or vitamin C (ascorbic acid). Dog food companies used to use ethoxyquin for preserving food. Ethoxyquin was originally developed as a rubber hardener; it was then used as an insecticide. Although it cannot legally be used to preserve human food (with the minor exception of chili powder) because there's some fairly convincing evidence that the stuff causes cancer, liver disease, and immune disorders, manufacturers have used it for years to preserve dog food. Because of increasing consumer pressure, the FDA announced in 1998 that ethoxyquin is not safe in dog food either. They have asked manufacturers to voluntarily stop using it.

4. Select food with the specific name of a meat (beef, chicken, turkey) as the first ingredient. Avoid foods whose label lists a generic "meat" or "poultry." Unfortunately, just because a product has "beef" as the first ingredient doesn't mean that the product is mostly beef. Some companies engage in a nefarious practice called "splitting." If they can possibly do so, they will divide the cereal products up into separate categories, like "rice" and then "brown rice." Added together, there may be more rice than beef. But because the companies are allowed to list them as separate ingredients, beef is listed first.

Dry Food (Kibble)

Kibble is a convenient, nutritionally adequate food for dogs. Dry food helps reduce tartar buildup on teeth, but not as much as actually brushing the teeth does. And it doesn't do anything for cleaning the canine teeth (the fangs), since chewing (if any) is done with the back teeth. In comparison with other food choices, dry food is the least expensive, largely because of its high grain content. Dry food tends to be low in fat, which is good if your dog is overweight or inactive. Don't be seduced by fancy colors and shapes, though. Shape doesn't matter, and the colors come from vegetable dye, not food nutrients.

Most, but not all, dry foods are preserved with BHA or BHT. Although BHA and BHT have been established as safe by the federal government, many people question this finding. If you don't wish to feed your dog food containing these preservatives, you can find some dry foods that don't use them. However, they are pricey and sometimes hard to locate.

Commercial kibble comes in several sizes. My own experience has been that the larger sizes are preferred by most Bulldogs, and some research has shown that larger-size kibble is less likely to be a factor in bloat, a dangerous emergency condition of the digestive system.

Some people like to feed their dogs a basic diet of kibble, with different added foods every day, like green beans, carrots, gravy, or canned meat. This plan gives your dog adequate nutrition and variety.

Canned Food

Although some canned dog food smells unpleasant to us (one reason most people prefer to serve kibble), most dogs prefer both the aroma and flavor of canned foods. In fact, some people serve such unappetizing dry fare that they have to anoint the stuff with canned food before their dogs will touch it. To find the best canned food for your dog, look for food containing whole meat, fish, or poultry as the first ingredient. Most lower-quality canned foods

Storing Food

Food stored improperly can become loaded with molds and other deadly toxins. To reduce the chances of your dog becoming a victim, be sure to use the freshest foods available. If you use a commercial food, check the manufacturing date. Do not buy in bulk; it may save you some money, but it's dangerous for your dog. Smaller bags get used more quickly and stay fresher longer.

Store the food in a dry, cool place away from sunlight. It's best if you keep the food in the house or some other place with a stable temperature. Temperature fluctuations can produce moisture in the food storage container that may lead to the development of mold or toxins. Most food should be kept in its original packaging or in a special airtight container. Don't use a plastic garbage can, even a clean one. These containers are often made of plastics that produce offensive or dangerous vapors.

If the food smells bad or if your dog suddenly refuses to eat it (while otherwise retaining his appetite), throw the stuff out, or take it back to the point of purchase for a refund.

Commercial foods provide a convenient way for you to feed your Bulldog.

have water as the first ingredient.

Unfortunately, the top canned foods often cannot be found at your supermarket. Instead, you must go to the manufacturer, a few pet specialty stores, or dog shows. This is because the high shelf rental space of most supermarkets is out of the reach of many small premium pet food manufacturers.

Canned food is much more expensive than kibble, and it is usually about 75 percent water. The maximum amount of water in canned foods in AAFCO-labeled products is 78 percent, unless the food is labeled as "gravy," "sauce," or "stew." In that case, water content can be even higher! Canned foods are also high in fat. They can be useful for mixing with dry food, however, as most dogs find them highly palatable. Dogs who have urinary tract infections often thrive better on canned dog foods than on kibble, mostly because of the increased water in canned foods.

Some canned dog foods contain grain products, while others have only meat. Whether or not grain products are good for dogs is controversial. The best canned foods use whole vegetables, not grain fractions like rice bran, rice flour, or brewers rice. Dogs do need a vegetable element in their diet, so if you feed a pure meat dinner, you should supplement it with dog biscuits or fresh vegetables.

Semi-Moist Food

Semi-moist food is about 25 percent water and can be just as high in sugar, in the form of corn syrup, beet pulp, sucrose, and caramel. Your dog does not need this stuff, which promotes obesity and tooth decay. The shelf life of these products is also lower than either canned or dry food.

People Food

Considering what the commercial pet food market is like, it's all right to feed your dog most food that is healthy for human beings. The old warnings about not feeding your dog table scraps were a masterpiece of propaganda served up with relish by dog food manufacturers. Dogs thrive on fresh vegetables, chicken, beef, and fish. Many dogs also like fruit, including apple slices, melon, banana, and berries. (I once had a dog who carefully picked blackberries from our bushes.) Low-fat plain yogurt and small amounts of cottage cheese are also delightful treats. Large amounts of dairy foods can be troublesome, however; most dogs don't have the necessary enzymes to process them.

Avoid cramming your dog with junk food you shouldn't be eating yourself, such as cookies, potato chips, chocolate (which is potentially toxic to dogs), hot dogs, and pickles. Many of these foods cause gastrointestinal upset, which can result in vomiting and diarrhea. This is especially likely with high-fat foods, to which your dog is probably not accustomed. The pancreas can really take a hit from these items, and your dog could get pancreatitis.

Homecooked Meals and Raw Diets

Nowadays, many people have opted to prepare their dog's diet at home. The advantages of homemade diets are obvious: You can tailor the diet to your own dog's particular needs, and you'll be using quality ingredients that don't include artificial preservatives and by-products. Although it is often claimed that diets prepared at home are more expensive than commercial ones, you can largely offset this factor by including healthy leftovers from your own meals.

Variety: The Spice of Life

The best single thing you can do to ensure that your dog is getting the nutrients he needs is to feed him a variety of different foods. This will not only make eating more pleasurable for him, but if you start early enough, it will help protect him from developing allergies. I also strongly urge you to supply your dog with something other than a steady diet of commercial foods. Well-chosen, lower-fat table scraps will not only reduce his risk of bloat (this is proven), but they can boost the quality of every meal by providing nutrients of the highest caliber (not by-products).

Treats fed in tiny quantities are an effective way to reward your Bulldog.

However, preparing a diet at home does require some training. The main dangers from such diets are a calcium/phosphorus imbalance and inadequate levels of calcium, copper, iodine, and certain vitamins, especially fat-soluble and some B vitamins. People who decide to feed their dogs a diet of fresh meat and vegetables without the bone must artificially supplement the food with a calcium source like bone meal. The exact amount is difficult to gauge. In addition, not all bone meal supplements are safe, and some contain dangerously high levels of lead. You are safer using a commercially prepared food or feeding raw meaty bones. Many excellent books have published recipes for healthy homemade diets that you can adopt for your own purposes.

If you decide to feed your dog raw meat, get the freshest cuts available. Because of the new interest in feeding raw diets, the FDA, which does not believe that raw diets are healthier than others, has issued the following guidelines for pet owners who want to try it with their dogs:

- Choose meat that has been approved for human consumption by the U.S. Department of Agriculture/Food Safety Inspection Service.
- Choose meat that comes from manufacturers who use

measures, such as irradiation, to prevent bacterial contamination of the meat.

- Choose meat from manufacturers who have implemented a hazard analysis and Critical Control Point program designed to pinpoint contamination sources and take action to prevent problems at these sources.
- Choose meats that have been frozen or freeze dried during shipping.
- Choose foods that include ground, not whole, bones.

Manufacturers should include guidelines for safe use with their products that instruct consumers to keep the products frozen until ready to use; thaw the product in a refrigerator or microwave; keep the product separate from other foods; refrigerate or discard unused product; and thoroughly wash working surfaces, utensils, hands, and any other items that touch the product.

A great deal has been written lately about the advantages of a raw diet. However, it is best to check with your vet before making any major decisions that may affect your dog's diet. There are some disadvantages to feeding your dog a raw diet, even if the meat supply is completely safe. Raw meat harbors organisms that can kill a dog. Common bacterial components of raw meat include campylobacterosis, *E. coli*, listeriosis, salmonellosis, trichinosis, and tapeworm. Protozoal infections are also possible. Cooking destroys those organisms. While it is true that cooking also destroys some important enzymes as well, dogs actually can make these enzymes themselves, just as humans can.

Don't let anyone talk you into a "natural diet" for your Bulldog without first consulting your veterinarian.

Grass Anyone?

If you catch your dog eating grass, he's not abnormal. Most dogs attempt to eat grass from time to time, although they can't digest it. No one knows why they do it. Some suggest dogs who eat grass have upset tummies and do so to make themselves throw up. Others suggest they just like the taste of the stuff.

Treats

Most people enjoy giving their dog treats, and it's a harmless enough activity, as long as you don't overfeed. However, some treats are definitely poor choices for your dog.

The popular use of cow hooves as dog treats is dangerous. Cow hooves are the number-one cause of broken teeth in dogs. Although wild dogs chew the hooves of recent kills, fresh hooves are much more pliable than the smoked variety commonly available in stores today.

Most Bulldogs like rawhide chews, sometimes too much. They chew them up like gum and then swallow them. The rawhide can stick in a Bulldog's throat. Even if he gets it down, it's not doing his digestive system any good. Some rawhide treats are basted with flavors that disagree with the canine digestive system, causing diarrhea. If you notice this, switch to plain rawhide treats, or omit them altogether. Dogs also have strong opinions when it comes to the perfect flavor in treats, but despite the recent plethora of melon, vanilla, and peanut butter delights, most dogs like liver. There's no accounting for taste.

If your dog is overweight, replace high-calorie treats with nutritious, crispy carrots, and add fresh vegetables like broccoli to your dog's dinner. Just as with humans, the key is a low-fat, high-fiber diet. Unless you're an expert on home-prepared foods, use a high-quality weight-loss commercial brand. The manufacturer has done the hard part by providing the correct amounts of vitamins and minerals.

Treats are not only a pleasant dietary interlude for your dog, but they are also (in tiny quantities) great for rewards during training. Bulldog like praise, but they do respond best to food.

Bones

Bones are naturally balanced sources of calcium and phosphorous, and dogs adore them. However, cooked bones are dangerous, because they can easily splinter and damage your dog's throat and digestive system. The sterilized bones you can buy in the store are very dangerous in this regard: They are unnaturally hard and can cause broken teeth. Whole, *fresh* bones are safer, but the best choice is to have the bones thoroughly ground and cooked. Raw bones may carry bacterial dangers of their own, but the nutritional advantages are without par. It is important that the bones be both fresh and meaty for your dog to benefit. Start your dog off gradually, and watch him closely. Dogs need to learn to eat bones properly.

Your best choices are raw chicken legs and wings, because these bones have a perfect calcium/phosphorus ratio. Beef and even turkey bones may be too hard.

The most dangerous consequence of bone consumption is a perforated intestine, which allows toxins to escape into the dog's system. When dogs chew bones, they splinter. Splintering bones can puncture the esophagus or stomach. Wild animals have to chew bones, and occasionally the bones can kill them. Don't risk your dog's life because you want him to be like White Fang. In fact, Bulldogs are nothing like White Fang, and their peculiar anatomical structure may make them especially vulnerable to choking. To reduce this risk, grind the bones thoroughly in a food grinder.

Foods to Avoid

Grapes and Raisins

Reports have recently implicated large amounts of grapes and raisins (between 9 ounces and 2 pounds {255 to 907g}) in acute kidney failure in dogs, although no one knows exactly why. The

kidney shutdown is so dramatic that aggressive treatment may be necessary to save your dog's life. Treatment for animals who have been poisoned by grapes and raisins includes:

- Administering activated charcoal. This helps prevent absorption of the toxic substance, whatever it is.
- Blood tests to evaluate kidney function.
- Hospitalization with intravenous fluids.

It's best to establish a set schedule for mealtime to avoid overfeeding your Bulldog.

If you decide to switch from one dog food brand to another, do so gradually over a period of a week or two, especially if your dog is a picky eater or has a sensitive stomach.
Try to avoid feeding your Bulldog anything containing soybean products, as Bulldogs often have trouble with this food.

Chocolate

Chocolate, especially baker's chocolate, can cause a range of problems, including cardiovascular difficulties and even seizures.

Onions

A quarter cup of onions can induce hemolytic anemia, a severe but usually temporary condition. Serious cases can even require a blood transfusion. Garlic has the same properties, but garlic in very small amounts probably does your dog some good. However, don't rely on garlic as a flea fighter.

Corn Cobs

Some people think it's interesting to watch their dogs deal with corn cobs. It's not. Dogs are not horses, and the cobs can impact the intestines.

FEEDING SCHEDULES

Feeding the Puppy

Young puppies (two to four months) need to eat four times a day, usually a high-quality kibble softened with some warm water. You can add yogurt, canola, corn oil, flaxseed oil, or cottage cheese for palatability. From four to six months, you may reduce the number of meals to three per day and reduce this to two meals a day at six months of age. At one year, some people start feeding once a day, although twice-daily feedings seem to please the dog more. Regardless of his age, your Bulldog should always have access to plenty of clean, fresh water.

Feeding the Adult Dog

Bulldogs reach adulthood between the ages of one year and eighteen months, and at this point they should be fed twice a day. If you are feeding a commercial food, choose one of high quality. If you are feeding kibble, you can top it off with a spoonful of yogurt or low-fat table scraps for added taste. Studies show this also helps prevent bloat.

Feeding the Senior Dog

As your Bulldog ages, he will become less active, and consequently he will need fewer calories. Although every individual is different, most Bulldogs acquire "seniority" at about eight years of age. If you are feeding a high-quality dog food, you can safely reduce the amount he eats. Less premium dog foods, however, contain just enough vitamins and minerals to keep your dog going at the amount indicated, so you will have to supplement with vitamins and minerals. Fish oil or glucosamine/chondroitin can be beneficial to many older animals.

However, if your senior dog seems to be doing just fine on his regular diet and he doesn't seem to be losing weight or condition, there's no reason at all to switch him just for the sake of switching. So-called senior dog foods are not required to meet any pre-determined standard, so two different "senior" dog foods may not be equivalent in the nutrition they provide.

Overall, keep in mind that older dogs have special dietary needs. One of the main ones is that they need more protein (unless they have kidney trouble) than young adults. They also benefit from arginine, an essential amino acid for the immune system; omega-3 fatty acids to keep their brains and nervous system in good repair; and less phosphorus to maintain health.

OBESITY

Obesity is the number-one nutritional disorder in American dogs. It can lead to problems such as diabetes and increase the negative impact of arthritis. Sixty percent of all adult dogs in the United States are overweight, a fact that affects their health, enjoyment of life, and ability to participate in normal dog activities. Bulldogs are particularly prone to obesity. No matter how much

Free Feeding Versus Scheduled Feeding

Mammals are programmed to be hungry all the time. In most cases, dogs should be fed on a schedule. It's hard to monitor how much a free-fed dog is actually consuming, and if you have more than one dog, you won't know who's getting the food. In addition, it has been shown that free feeding is very strongly linked with obesity. If you want a fit dog, feed him a proper amount at scheduled times; don't let him decide for himself. Dogs don't make very good decisions about these things. The genetic heritage of dogs encourages them to gorge when food is available, and even though your Bulldog hasn't been out hunting caribou in a long, long, long time, his genes don't know that. Where food is concerned, he thinks he's still a wolf.

fun it is to feed your dog, and no matter how much he enjoys eating, remember: Obesity will shorten his life.

Obesity is defined as being 10 to 25 percent above the ideal weight for your dog. Look at your Bulldog from above: He should resemble an hourglass. Too much bulge in the waist indicates that your dog needs to be put on a diet. If you run your thumbs along your dog's spine, you should be able to feel each rib. If you must put pressure on the rib cage to feel the ribs, he's overweight. (If you can actually see your dog's ribs, he's too thin.) When viewed from the side, you should see a "tucked-up" waist.

Although most cases of obesity are due to the fatal combination of overfeeding and underexercising, in a few instances a medical condition like hypothyroidism or insulin imbalance could be at fault. Don't put your dog on a weight-loss program until you check with your veterinarian to make sure there are no underlying medical problems.

The best way to control your dog's weight is to provide him with the proper amount of food for his ideal size. Your vet can help you to determine that. I know you enjoy feeding your dog treats, but they add weight. If you do like to treat your dog, cut down on the meals proportionately, or give low-calorie treats like carrot slivers.

In some cases, you may want to resort to a commercial low-calorie food. Pick one that includes specific weight-loss directions.

How Much Is Too Much?

Research at the Ralston Purina Pet Care Center indicates that an inactive 50-pound adult dog requires 1,450 calories a day in the summer. (That's your Bulldog, all right!) The same dog requires 1,800 calories during moderate work or training and 2,160 calories when performing heavy work. Don't worry about these latter figures—your Bulldog won't be doing any heavy work. It's important to remember that these calorie requirements are for dogs in general, not for Bulldogs in particular, let alone yours. Age, temperature, and activity level are important qualifications. It's just not possible to precisely determine how many calories a particular dog will actually require. Luckily, you don't need to know exactly how many calories your dog actually needs. Just keep an eye on him. If he starts looking pudgy, reduce his intake, and if he starts looking too thin, increase his intake.

An adult Bulldog should only be fed twice a day to prevent him from becoming overweight.

If you feed a dog according to the regular feeding directions, he won't lose weight. Regular feeding directions are designed to maintain a dog's weight.

Another way to keep your dog's weight in check is to provide him with plenty of healthy exercise. Dogs like this option much better than cutting down on their chow, too. If you are starting an exercise weight-loss program for your dog, check with your vet before embarking on anything strenuous.

C h a p t e r

5

GROOMING
Your Bulldog

lthough grooming your dog well will certainly make him feel like a Westminster champion, it does more than improve his looks. It is also a great way to keep him in good health and cement your bond with him. Pretty impressive for a few minutes of brushing a couple of times a week! Grooming your dog puts him in the center of attention, where all Bulldogs long to be. You not only get to make him over, but you also get to check him out for bumps, growths, sores, and bruises. It's a first-line defense against disease. In addition, by removing dead and dirty hair and stimulating the skin, grooming also aids your Bulldog in avoiding skin infections and irritations. Spreading natural oils throughout the skin helps the coat retain its luster. In addition, well-groomed dogs look and smell better and are consequently more likely to be included in family activities.

BRUSHING

Most Bulldogs love to be gently brushed, so do it about three times a week, using a soft bristle or rubber brush. You can get away with once a week or even every other week, but more frequent brushing is best. The general practice is to start brushing at the head and then work your way down the back to the tail. The sides should follow, finishing with the legs. Use short, quick strokes, and don't press hard. While you brush, angle the bristles away from the skin so that you don't irritate it.

It is important to get your dog used to the idea of brushing. It is a strange feeling to a dog and can stress him out if he is the nervous type. Begin gradually if your dog seems unacquainted with the idea.

Types of Brushes

Many kinds of brushes are available for Bulldogs, and luckily, it's not a big deal if you

pick the wrong one. Some popular brushes for Bulldogs include a pliable rubber brush with several soft spikes or nubs, the slicker brush (with flexible metal pins), and a rubber hound mitt. The pliable rubber brush and slicker brush will both strip out the dead hair from the coat, but the slicker is best for the undercoat, and the pliable rubber brush is best for the top coat. The hound mitt will finish it off with a nice polish to the Bulldog's short coat.

How to Brush Your Bulldog

Begin at the back of the head, using the slicker brush with gentle, flowing strokes. The aim is to remove the dead hair and dirt from the undercoat. Then repeat with the slicker. Some groomers recommend beginning at the rear and brushing gently *against* the hair growth pattern to stimulate the skin and remove loose hair. Then brush along the hair growth pattern and follow with a rubdown or polishing with the hound mitt. Use whatever method works best for you and your dog, but always finish by praising him like mad.

BATHING

A well-brushed dog doesn't need a daily bath, but most people err on the side of bathing their dogs less often than they should. Bathing your dog correctly with a high-quality dog shampoo with conditioner will not strip away his natural oils any more than washing your hair every day does yours. In fact, a buildup of these oils can give your dog a pretty heady odor, so bathe your Bulldog as often as you find necessary. Bathing keeps your dog clean and is a great prevention against hot spots.

You can bathe your Bulldog in the bathtub or utility sink—in fact, anywhere that you have a supply of warm water and can restrain your dog. If you use a tub, put down a rubber mat; enamel is slippery stuff, and your dog could slide and injure himself. Tubs are also a real strain on the back. If your shower doesn't have a hand-held spray attachment, get one. This inexpensive, easily installed device will pay for itself in terms of comfort the very first time you use it. You might also consider using a mesh drain liner for collecting all that pesky hair that falls out.

Supplies

Before beginning, gather your supplies. A tearless shampoo for dogs or humans is best. You can even buy canine shampoos and

Did You Know?

Dog hair differs from human hair in a lot of ways. For example, dogs have compound hair follicles, which means that as many as 20 hairs can pop up from each pore. Human beings have only one hair per follicle. In addition, dogs have not one but three different kinds of hairs: guard hairs (longer and coarser), undercoat (soft and thick), and medium hairs. Different breeds have different concentrations of each kind, but each individual hair follicle produces all three kinds of hair, usually one guard hair and several finer hairs. Although the hair follicles are living cells, hair itself is dead, no matter what they say in shampoo commercials.

Grooming Supplies

The following grooming supplies will keep your Bulldog healthy and looking his best.

- Brushes
- Shampoo
- Cotton-tip applicators and cotton balls
- Baby powder
- Mustard squirt bottle (clean and empty, of course) to squirt cleaner into the hard-to-access wrinkles, especially under the nose rope
- Nail clippers or a grinder
- Canine toothbrush and toothpaste
- Grooming table (while not a necessity, it may come in handy)

rinses designed especially for the color of your dog (red, white, etc.) at grooming shops, pet supply stores, and dog shows. You should also have some cotton batting, cotton-tipped swabs, and mineral oil or eye ointment. Put a drop of this in the eyes before you begin; it will help keep out the shampoo. Also, place cotton in the dog's ears to keep water from running in them.

How to Bathe Your Bulldog

Soak the dog completely, up and down, front and back. Dogs hate hot water, so make the bath water lukewarm. That's warm enough to get him clean and cool enough so he won't complain, at least not too much. Start at the neck and work backward, making sure not to miss the areas between the toes, under the tail, and the genitals. You can also wash the face gently with a washcloth and a bit of shampoo. You must take special care of the Bulldog's wrinkles and tail pocket! Then wash the nose and outside of the ears.

Follow with a conditioner rinse if desired. Then rinse like mad, especially around those wrinkles—you don't want soap drying in there and irritating the skin. It should take twice as long to rinse the dog as it did to wash him. Then rinse him again. Towel dry, and clean the inside of the ears with a washcloth after you take out the cotton batting. You can also let your dog air dry at this point, or use

To bathe your Bulldog, soak him with lukewarm water and shampoo him all over.

a hair dryer designed for dogs, being careful not to use one around the head. (Some human ones are too hot.) Keep the dog inside until he's dry. (This may take a couple of hours.) Make sure the wrinkles get dry, too! Wet wrinkles can lead to infection.

WRINKLE CARE

Bulldog wrinkles need frequent cleaning. They are prone to irritation and can collect dirt and debris. It's not enough to clean them only when you're bathing the dog. The older Bulldogs get, the more they tend to wrinkle, so you'll need to step it up as your pet ages. You can't go wrong by washing those wrinkles every day at the same time you brush his teeth. Hot, humid weather causes more trouble because it produces conditions that allow bacteria to accumulate.

Depending on the condition of the wrinkles, you can use a cloth with plain water or you can add a bit of baby shampoo. An easier solution is to use baby wipes with aloe and lanolin. Try squirting the cleansing material into the wrinkle with a clean plastic mustard squeezer. The nose wrinkle needs special attention; if it looks irritated, use a soothing cream or ointment. You can apply the ointment with a child's toothbrush.

TEAR STAINS (EPIPHORA)

Some dogs do not have proper tear drainage. This can result from clogged lacrimal ducts, or more commonly, a conformation that prevents the tears from opening the duct. It can also occur because the tears that are produced are too thick to flow into the duct opening.

Reddish-brown tear stains occur most noticeably on dogs with light-colored coats and heavy wrinkles. The color is due to normal facial bacteria mixing with the tears. In pronounced cases, a crust forms in the corner of the eye and over the skin, sometimes even resulting in small ulcers. Some stains are just the result of hair near the eyes wicking moisture from the eyes. Other stains are related to diet, health, and genetics. (Mother dogs with tear stains are likely to have offspring with the same problem.) The damp, heavily wrinkled face of a Bulldog provides a good ground for the growth of bacteria and yeast, including the infamous "red yeast," which not only looks bad but smells bad, too. The red yeast can even infect the tear ducts, which increases the problem. Unless the tear staining comes from a clogged tear duct, there's really nothing that can be done to prevent it from occurring.

Tear stains present a special grooming challenge. To do the most effective job, try to determine the source. (You may need a

Clean your Bulldog's wrinkles daily to remove dirt and debris that may gather there.

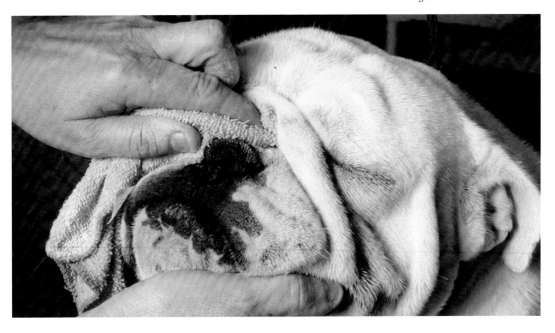

veterinarian's advice.) Some commercial products are available, and you can also try to bleach the stains out with a mixture of 1 tablespoon of hydrogen peroxide, a little milk of magnesia, and enough cornstarch to make a paste. Other people have had success with a boric acid ointment. Spread the stuff on top of the stain; you should see the stain disappear or at least lighten up after several weeks. Take care not to get anything in the dog's eyes.

Some people have actually consulted veterinary ophthalmologists for recalcitrant cases, and to help some animals, have opted for eye duct surgery that increases tear capacity.

Some people just give up and have the vet or groomer cut their dog's nails. While this is the easy way out, it's expensive and increases your dog's stress level. Nail trimming is a skill that every competent dog owner should learn.

NAIL CARE

Keep your Bulldog's nails in good repair. This means that you should clip them every other week or so, less often if your Bulldog walks a lot on hard pavement. Keep your Bulldog's nails trimmed short enough so that they don't touch the floor when he walks. Long nails can eventually lead to a deformed foot. If the nails are very hard, soak them in warm water for 15 minutes before you begin.

Types of Clippers

Use good quality canine (not human) dog nail clippers, either a scissor or guillotine type. Either kind of clipper works fine as long as you keep the equipment sharp. Dull blades don't work, and they will hurt your dog. Human toenail clippers aren't strong or sharp enough for canine nails. Most groomers consider the guillotine-type clippers the best and easiest to operate. However, if your Bulldog tends to have cracked nails, a guillotine-type clipper can crush them. Scissors-type clippers tend to be stronger and sharper, and it's easier, in my experience, to estimate where the quick of the nail is.

You can also use an electric nail grinder. Some dogs may prefer a grinder once they get used to the noise. You just need to watch that the grinder doesn't get too hot.

How to Clip Your Bulldog's Nails

Nail clipping can be stressful for both the Bulldog and his owner. Owners worry about clipping the nails too short, and their fear is translated to the dog. Try to make this experience as pleasant as possible for the dog. To do this right, you'll need to control him, something that's best accomplished with a grooming table, although some people sit right on the floor with their dogs. You may need an assistant, especially at first, because many Bulldogs simply detest having their nails done. Try distracting your Bulldog with a bit of peanut butter or other chewy treat while you're grooming him to take his mind off the process. If you don't make too big a deal of it, he won't either.

When clipping, avoid the quick, which is the live part of the nail. You can easily see the quick on a white-nailed dog, but if your dog has black nails, just cut to the curve. (If the nails are very long, you'll have to do only a little bit at a time, since the quick will continue to grow longer and longer.) To trim your puppy's nails, hold one rear paw in one hand firmly but without squeezing. (Most dogs are less fussy about their rear paws, so it's often easier to begin with one of them.) Press lightly enough to separate the toes, and clip each nail right below the quick. That's the part that hurts. If you leave any ragged edges, a touch with a nail file will polish

Your Bulldog's nails should be clipped every other week if he does not wear them down naturally on pavement.

the nails off nicely. If you happen to clip a nail too short, simply apply some styptic powder to the nail to stem bleeding. Just take a pinch of it between your thumb and forefinger and press against the cut nail. If you're caught without any powder, you can try using a little cornstarch or flour in the same manner. Don't make a big deal of it.

The pads of the feet also deserve care. As tough as they appear, they can be torn, caked with tar, or embedded with thorns. Trim the hair between the pads, also. Long hair can become caked with gunk and form an impenetrable mass that is painful to your dog. In serious cases, a foot infection could develop. Tar can be removed from paw pads by applying petroleum jelly or mineral oil to the affected area. Follow with warm water and a mild soap. Never use turpentine or paint thinner to remove tar.

NOSE CARE

The Bulldog's nose tends to dry out. Fix it by smearing some petroleum jelly on the nose regularly.

TAIL CARE

Some Bulldogs have their tail set in a "pocket." If this is the case with your dog, you'll need to clean the pocket often since all kinds of debris can accumulate in there. Apply an ointment or powder when finished.

DENTAL CARE

As you might expect, the Bulldog's mouth is pretty important. Dogs need a mouth to eat, drink, groom themselves, cool off, and communicate. It's up to you to take good care of it!

Dog teeth are subject to the same dental problems we humans have: plaque, tartar, and gum and tooth disease. Plaque is the sticky stuff that covers the teeth. It's a delightful mix of bacteria, saliva, food particles, and dead cells from the mouth lining. It is constantly deposited on the teeth and gums and can harden into tartar in less than two days. Once tartar forms, it makes a structure to let even more plaque accumulate, and so on. It's a vicious cycle for sure, and one that leads to periodontal disease. Fortunately, preventing periodontal disease is as simple as brushing your dog's teeth every day.

You should brush your dog's teeth about as often as you brush your own. It takes about the same length of time. Not only is it healthy and a way to bond with your dog, it's also a good chance for you to carefully examine your Bulldog's mouth every day for tartar buildup, swellings, and broken teeth. It's amazing what you may find in there. When you brush your dog's teeth properly, you are removing plaque in the groove below the gum line where chew toys and doggy treats don't reach. You can also rinse your dog's mouth with an oral rinse, or you can use dental wipes every day.

To accustom your dog to having his teeth brushed, start by putting a little of the canine toothpaste on your finger and just letting him lick it. Soon you'll be able to run your finger, perhaps covered with a bit of soft cloth, around his teeth. In no time at all, you can graduate to a toothbrush!

Dogs can get cavities, but they are relatively rare. The cause is usually a high-sugar diet, so lay off the sugary snacks. You will also need to take your Bulldog for a regular professional dental cleaning. The vet will anesthetize him, flush out the mouth, and clean the teeth with both hand-held and ultrasonic scalers to remove all tartar from above and below the gum line. She will polish the teeth as well—not because it makes them whiter, but because polishing removes microscopic scratches on the teeth that make a good home for plaque and tartar buildup. You can slightly reduce your dog's chances of developing dental disease by feeding a hard kibble diet. Certain dog chews and toys such as Nylabones may also help remove plaque, but they do not replace daily tooth brushing.

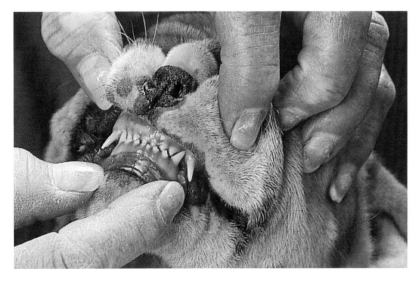

A dog's mouth is subject to the same problems that humans have, so it's important to inspect it frequently for signs of disease.

6

TRAINING *and* BEHAVIOR
of Your Bulldog

ulldogs respond well only to positive training. These are independent, smart dogs who do not blossom under punishment or harsh treatment of any kind. Their tough exterior hides a tender soul. They also respond best in a situation when trust has been established between them and their owners. Positive training may not be the fastest way to get the results you want, but it's the best way because you will build rather than damage your relationship.

The earlier you start training your dog, the better, as young dogs have fewer bad habits to overcome. You should concentrate your first training efforts on building trust. For your Bulldog to have the best learning experience possible, you need to create a safe environment. Focus on praise rather than punishment, and view the training process as teaching. Don't expect your Bulldog to turn into Rin Tin Tin, though. This is not an "obedience breed," and your Bulldog is not going to wait breathlessly while you tell him what to do. Figure out what you really want him to learn and then proceed slowly, making sure he has achieved one skill before advancing to the next.

To get the most positive response from your Bulldog, try to figure out what motivates him most. It might be food, play, or praise. Just remember that your Bulldog is an individual who will respond in a unique way to training. In addition, reward a desired behavior the second it occurs, not five minutes later. Bulldogs live in the now.

While dogs understand many more everyday words than we previously thought, they are more attuned to your tone of voice than to your vocabulary. Your tone should match your meaning. If you praise your dog in a dark or unhappy tone of voice, he won't get the message. If you scold him in a cheerful way, he won't get that, either.

SOCIALIZATION

If your puppy is between 4 and 12 months old, he is in the socialization period, his once-in-a-lifetime opportunity to learn how to play well with others and respond positively to new things. If you fail to take advantage of this period, it's very possible that your dog will be doomed to an antisocial, fearful life.

Around the middle of this period is the so-called fear period, the time where in the wild, the pups would first leave their dens to encounter the world. It was a dangerous world, so puppies developed a cautious attitude toward its exploration. Today, puppies have the same cautious instincts, so it is very important during this time for your Bulldog to have as few fearful experiences as possible. These negative experiences can become embedded in his psyche.

To this end, it's wise to introduce your pup to new things only gradually. Let him meet other dogs and people a few at a time. Don't just plunge him into a large group of strangers. You know your pup best, so gauge by his attitude how ready he is to expand his horizons. Your Bulldog's adventures might include puppy kindergarten, puppy play groups, your friends' houses, and pet supply stores.

If your dog seems confident, introduce him in a positive way to nail clippers, the vacuum cleaner, hair dryer, and air-conditioning unit. If he learns that noise doesn't equal pain, he'll feel more secure. In addition, take your Bulldog on walks so that he can encounter people of every age, dress, race, and accoutrement, including wheelchairs, canes, and walkers. Babies, children, people in uniform, and people with beards and hats should certainly be part of the routine as well.

HOUSETRAINING

Puppies will have accidents, just like kids do. Humans are supposed to be smarter than dogs, but many children are often not toilet trained until the age of three—yet some owners expect their puppy to be perfect at four months! If you change those unrealistic expectations, you'll save yourself a lot of grief.

If you're oblivious to what's going on until your puppy actually starts eliminating, don't panic. It's not the end of the world. If you start screaming, you'll convince your dog that he has done something awful (not that eliminating in the house is awful, but

Clicker Training

One popular way to train dogs uses a method called "clicker training." Clicker training is a form of operant conditioning using a clicker as a marker to help your dog identify a behavior that produces a reward (usually small treats). In clicker training, you don't give a command until after a behavior is reliably repeated. You use the clicker to "capture" the correct behavior.

that eliminating altogether is awful). Because your Bulldog can't stop eliminating, he'll start hiding it. The key is to act calmly and to promptly teach the puppy the nuanced lesson that eliminating *outside* is award-winning; eliminating inside is nonrewarding.

To socialize your Bulldog puppy, gradually introduce him to new dogs and people.

Keys to Successful Housetraining

The keys to successful housetraining include:

- Containment
- Reward
- Attention
- Patience
- Scheduling

Containment

Containment is synonymous with crating your Bulldog. Should you use a crate? In a word, yes. A crate is you and your dog's best friend. Containment is the essence of housetraining, but it should be used in moderation. First of all, forcing a dog to stay in a crate too long defeats the very purpose of crate training. After all, he can only hold it so long, and if left in a crate for an extended period of time, your poor Bulldog will be forced to urinate in it. This, in turn, breaks down the natural inhibitions he has about urinating in his den. Before long, you'll have more problems than before.

Practice putting your puppy in the crate for brief periods when you are home with him. Give him a toy or snack to work on while he's there. This will help him associate the crate with a pleasant place to be.

It's a dog world axiom that a puppy up to eight months of age can "hold it" as many hours as his age in months, plus one. Thus, a two-month-old puppy should be able hold it for three hours. However, puppies need plenty of exercise and opportunities to explore their surroundings. The idea of keeping an eight-month-old dog in a crate all day is repulsive. Even if your Bulldog somehow valiantly manages to hang on longer than is good for him, you may be courting future disasters in the form of bladder stones.

I believe that four hours is the maximum time a dog should be left in a crate. There is more to consider here than whether or not the dog will urinate in the house. You need to consider his psychological needs and his need for exercise. Dogs are complex creatures, and the highly intelligent, curious Bulldog cannot bear the attendant psychological deprivation that naturally goes along with long periods of being crated.

If you must keep your dog in a crate for longer periods of time, be absolutely sure to exercise him before and after his period of confinement. If this means getting up earlier in the morning to go for a walk with your Bulldog, please do so. If you must be gone for longer periods, please help your dog by hiring a dog walker to take care of his potty needs.

Reward

When your puppy succeeds in accomplishing his mission, praise him lavishly. A sedate pat on the head and a "Good boy, Warren!" won't suffice. Go crazy with joy and exuberant praise. If you have time, let him play a bit before you bring him inside. This will act as a further reward. If you take him directly inside afterward, he'll respond by delaying the precipitating event as long as possible outside, since he's undoubtedly enjoying himself

Attention

One mark of the astute dog owner is figuring out the signs of impending elimination. While the puppy is still learning how to tell you he wants to go, it's up to you to figure it out on your own. Can you do it? Are you smarter than your Bulldog?

Did You Know?

You're doing your Bulldog a great favor if you enroll him in an elementary training or socialization class. Look for one that operates using rewards rather than punishment. Not only will your Bulldog learn manners, but more importantly, you'll learn a few things yourself. This is also a great opportunity for you to bond with your dog. You can usually enter your puppy at three months, with "graduation" at five months. These classes are valuable because they help your puppy develop socialization skills with people and other dogs.

Common signs of an upcoming event include circling the floor, paw or mouth licking, and whining. The last behavior is especially useful, and one you want to encourage, because you don't have to be in the same room as your dog to get the signal.

Often, puppies don't think of eliminating until it's an emergency situation, so you may want to simply pick up your dog and carry him out. This will prevent an accident happening on the way to the door, a fairly common occurrence.

Patience

Be patient. Your Bulldog puppy has a tiny bladder and almost no bladder or anal sphincter control, and he won't have control until he is at least four months old. When you put these two factors together, it soon becomes clear that puppy housetraining is a job that requires your constant attention. But take my word for it—if you do everything (or even most things) correctly in the beginning, the entire process will not take long. Remember that you are dealing with an intelligent and eager-to-please pet. If you do your part and make it clear what you want, your Bulldog will do his part. A puppy is housetrained when he knows what you want and makes every effort to comply. Simply because he can't wait as long as an older dog doesn't mean he's not trained; it means he has reached his limit.

Scheduling

Keep to a schedule. Eight-week-old puppies should go out every couple of hours. Puppies new to the household should go out even more frequently, as nervousness and excitement stimulate their bladders. Most adult dogs can be left alone for eight hours, but this is variable, just as it is with people. Don't leave food out in a dish all day long for your unhousetrained dog; it can mess up his schedule.

When your Bulldog understands that he can depend on you to take him out at regular times (dogs have clocks in their heads), he'll be more inclined to wait for that moment. If he doesn't have a clue when or if you're going to take him out, he may feel as if he has nothing to wait for.

A strict schedule should apply to eating times as well, because the two events—eating and elimination—are connected. If you have to leave your dog alone all day and he can't hold it, think about hiring a dog-walking or pet-sitting service. Or take some of that unused vacation time. Your Bulldog will appreciate the company, too.

It's best to select a particular spot you want your Bulldog to use as his private bathroom. You can reduce lawn stains that way, and also reduce the chances you yourself will step in something unpleasant.

How to Housetrain Your Bulldog

In order to successfully housetrain your Bulldog puppy, you must go outside with him. Do not just let him out to wander around aimlessly in the yard. If you do that, you won't know whether he has succeeded in his mission or not. If left outside on his own, your puppy will undoubtedly find it so interesting and exciting that he'll completely forget why he is outdoors in the first place. A less adventuresome puppy may simply sit down on the back steps and wait for you to join him. He'd rather be with you, anyway, and you accompanying him will make his outdoor duty seem less like an exile and more like a walk. But it isn't a walk. Don't allow him to toddle off everywhere smelling everything; keep him focused. I find it helps to encourage the puppy to walk in circles in the area you have selected as his bathroom. Praise him when he succeeds.

If you cannot teach your Bulldog to bark when he wants in or out, you can buy a doggie doorbell designed to prevent scratching. A pad can be placed on either side of your door at your dog's height. When your pet touches the pad, a built-in wireless transmitter will activate a door chime. You can also install a pet door. Other owners train their dogs to come and sit in front of them when they wish to go out.

When Accidents Happen

If an accident does occur, assume it *is* an accident, and don't go ballistic or scold your puppy. If you're too late to catch him, clean it up and forget about it. Your dog certainly has! Just try to be more attentive next time.

When cleaning, use enzyme cleaners that will neutralize the scent. It's usually best to clean up the mess out of sight of the puppy. Never rub your Bulldog's nose in his excrement; this is a

On hot summer days, your Bulldog will need to drink more water, and as a result, he'll need to go out more frequently. Don't take away his water dish in the hopes that he won't need to urinate as much. You'll succeed only in tormenting the poor creature with thirst. However, feeding your dog dry food rather than canned food will reduce his need to urinate frequently.

form of punishment that is dirty, cruel, and ineffective. And of course, you should never strike your Bulldog for any reason, least of all for a household accident. Doing so will only make him afraid of you and will do nothing to change the behavior.

Scolding your puppy after the fact only confuses him. He'll assume you are scolding him for eliminating altogether, not for eliminating in the wrong place. Since he can't stop himself from eliminating, he'll be forced to find secret little places to accomplish his mission. Then you'll be wandering all around the house, wrinkling your nose and exclaiming, "I *know* there's an accident around here somewhere…where is it?"

Keeping your puppy focused on the task at hand will help him become housetrained more quickly.

I also have a suspicion that scolding a dog for eliminating inappropriately encourages him to start eating the evidence itself. If this occurs, you'll have not one but two unfortunate habits to discourage. Some dogs acquire this awful habit (called coprophagia) anyway, but scolding a dog for a housetraining mistake can be a factor in producing it, especially in cases where dogs consume their *own* feces.

Correcting a Mistake

If you catch your Bulldog in the act (not afterward), grab a leash (you should have several, one hanging on each available doorknob), and cry, "Out, out!" Then race outside with him and praise him for finishing outdoors. If you actually pick up the puppy, he will probably stop peeing while you're en route, but I can't guarantee it.

Cleaning Up

If the accident occurs on a rug, use an enzyme cleaner and follow the directions on the label. Unfortunately, if you try to clean the spot with a more conventional cleaner first, the enzyme cleaner will not be as effective.

Some people tout the advantages of household vinegar for cleaning up urine. This works very well if you don't mind a spot smelling of dog pee and vinegar. In reality, vinegar does not remove dog urine odors from carpet. Your best bet is one of the newer enzyme cleaners on the market that really do work. Never use an ammonia-based cleaner to remove a dog urine stain. Because ammonia smells like urine to a dog, you'll only succeed in making him think that that spot is a good place to eliminate.

When Urination Is More Than Just Urination

Unlike human beings (at least unlike most civilized human beings), dog have discovered a use for urination that goes far beyond simple elimination. This is what I call the urination subtext. It's up to you as the more intelligent mammal to figure out what your Bulldog is trying to tell you when he eliminates.

Submissive Urination

This is a commonly observed behavior in rescued dogs, shy dogs, puppies, and in new dogs introduced into a household where there are dominant dogs. Not all house soiling is the result of incomplete housetraining. When submissive urination occurs, a shy dog is responding to perceived threats by urinating on the floor. The key here is "perceived threat." *You* may think you are just "disciplining" your dog, but he figures that you are trying to hurt him. Some dogs are so submissive that they urinate even when a person just approaches them. In some cases, the dog crouches or even rolls over on his back while urinating. What you are seeing is fear, pure and simple.

Submissive urination is a natural action. Wild dogs urinate submissively before pack leaders. Unfortunately, while submissive urination has a mollifying effect on the canine pack leader, it usually leads to the opposite response in human owners, who become even angrier. Then the dog thinks, "Hmm, my owner must not have seen me urinate. I'd better do it again." This is the kind of miscommunication that can lead to real trouble.

Consider a Litter Box

Even though we have become accustomed to thinking that dogs have to eliminate outdoors, most of us have been surprised by enough presents on the floor to know that dogs don't always share our point of view.

In some cases, a litter box can be the perfect answer to housetraining woes. Here are some examples:

- When there's a blizzard outside, with 3 feet of snow on the ground.
- When you live 10 stories up and you can't face dragging your Bulldog outside at 3:00 a.m.
- When either you or your dog is ill, old, or arthritic, and the daily outside voyage is a little too much.
- When you're going to be gone for hours and you know it's not fair to ask the dog to "hold it."

Canine litter pans are on the market now, so all you have to do is teach your dog to use one. Line the litter box with something similar to the surface your dog is used to. If it's asphalt, you may have a problem, but you can substitute a clay-based litter.

Introduce your dog to the litter pan at times when he's most likely to need it, like after waking up or after meals. If you're lucky, he'll use it immediately and you can go wild with praise. Even some curious sniffing around the pan is worth some verbal encouragement from you. You can also try taking the litter pan outside with you and encouraging your Bulldog to use it out there. When he gets the idea, start bringing the pan closer to the house until he's litter trained.

Luckily, the solution for submissive urination is simple: Stop punishing the dog. Instead of penalizing negative actions, reward positive behavior. If your dog is a submissive urinator, ignore the action completely. Don't scold, glare, yell, strike him, or even call attention to the fact that he urinated. Instead, ignore the mess, walk out of the room, and clean it up later. Specifically, avoid eye contact with the miscreant. Dogs regard eye contact as either a threat, or in sophisticated dogs, as a reward—and you don't want to give either message! The less attention your Bulldog receives in response to his behavior, the less likely he will be to repeat it. It may take a while, but gradually your submissive dog will acquire the self-confidence to rid himself of the habit.

To avoid submissive urination, keep your greetings to the dog low key. Approach from the side rather than from the front. Don't tower over him any more than you can help until he regains some confidence. Crouch down, lean back, open your arms, and call the dog to you. Avoid looking directly into his eyes. Stroke him on the chest or under the chin, not on the top of the head. When he responds with positive, assured actions, pet and play with him. Remember that dogs who submissively urinate have self-confidence problems, and these dogs should never be punished.

Territorial Marking

Unneutered males often develop the unpleasant habit of marking their territory by lifting their leg and urinating on walls or furniture. This may be more likely to occur if there's another dog around, either a female in heat or a male the unneutered male perceives as a challenge. (Even dogs who don't mark in their homes almost certainly will do so outside.) When a dog marks, he releases only a small amount of urine (as opposed to regular urination).

Altered males may also exhibit this behavior, although less frequently. I have even observed this behavior (although usually outdoors) in dominant females. It may also crop up if there has been a change in family structure and the dominant partner leaves. In a few cases, insecure or anxious dogs will also mark, perhaps feeling that it empowers them. Marking is due to the presence of the testosterone hormone.

To a lesser extent, the same behavior applies to defecation. I have seen many an unneutered male defecate directly in front of a rival, especially when the latter was penned up and unable to retaliate.

If your house marker is not neutered, the best cure is to have him neutered as soon as you can. If that is not possible, treat the marking problem the same as you would a regular housetraining lapse. Say, "No," and get the dog outside immediately. Older, more confident dogs may be firmly scolded.

Exuberant or Excitement Urination

Sometimes your puppy is so excited to see you that he just can't hold it another instant. This behavior is not really

When It's Time to See the Vet

If your Bulldog eliminates in a way you think isn't normal — too much, too little, odd posture, straining or discomfort, or odd places or circumstances — take him to your vet first for a thorough exam. All kinds of medical conditions could cause the problem.

Certain medical conditions manifest themselves by increased urination, urinary incontinence, or difficulty urinating. Elderly females often "leak," especially at night while sleeping. Cushing's disease, bladder stones, chronic kidney failure, brain or spinal cord injury, diabetes, and certain medications can all affect urination patterns.

If you notice any changes or abnormalities in your Bulldog's elimination habits, note them carefully and consult your veterinarian. Bring a sample to the office with you if possible.

Lavishly praise your Bulldog when he executes a training command well.

related to submissive urination, although at first glance they may seem similar. However, a dog who experiences excitement urination doesn't crouch or act submissive. He's just thrilled. It occurs mostly at playtime and is characteristic of dogs under one year of age. These dogs become so involved with their activity that they just can't hold it any longer. This problem usually disappears on its own as the dog gains more control over his natural functions.

The cure for excitement urination is much the same as for submissive urination. The best way to react to this behavior is not to react at all. If you return your Bulldog's jubilant greeting too enthusiastically, he won't receive the correct message. Be calm, nonchalant even, as you greet your dog. Walk into another room and examine your mail. In a few minutes, after the dog is a little calmer, you may pet him and greet him. Then take him outside to eliminate.

BASIC TRAINING

Modern dogs need to be mannerly household pets and citizens of the world. A trained dog is a pleasure to be around and will be included more often in activities than will an ill-trained dog. Good training can also save your dog's life.

There is a difference between general good behavior around the house and formal obedience. Many dogs are a joy to have around

Keep initial training sessions short and fun—your Bulldog will enjoy them more!

the house, even though they can't fetch or heel. Bulldogs are much better (usually) at being well mannered than well trained. However, it's certainly not impossible to train your Bulldog to perform routine commands like sitting, lying down, and heeling.

One way to make your training more successful is to make use of "treats," "bait," or "lures," different names for the same thing. When you are first teaching a particular skill to your dog, use a treat every time. As your Bulldog learns what you want of him, you can start handing out treats more infrequently—not every time. Studies show that animals actually learn better when rewards are offered intermittently, after they understand what is desired of them.

All first training sessions should be indoors, where there are fewer distractions.

Watch Me

This is the basic focus command. If your dog isn't paying any attention to you, he won't be able to learn anything. Help him focus by using positive reinforcement and treats. This doesn't mean that you should give your dog food every time he looks at you. It means that he should always consider it as a viable possibility. Once he learns that "watch me!" brings praise or even a reward, he'll be anxious to learn what you have to say next.

To teach "watch me!" say the words and hold a treat near your face. If your Bulldog doesn't see the treat at first, you may have to start to lower it toward his field of vision. He'll catch on soon.

The number of times you do anything should depend on the age, training, and maturity of your Bulldog. Stop while he is still having fun! Usually a minute or two is long enough.

Leave It

This simple command is a lifesaver. Young dogs are forever getting into garbage, diapers, and expensive shoes. Start teaching your Bulldog by waiting until he is chewing on an object that he really doesn't care that much about. (It should also be one that's not important to you, either.) As he's chewing, go up to your dog, and say, "Leave it!" Offer him a treat in exchange. Make sure the treat is preferable to what he's chewing. Bits of bacon and cheese are great favorites. Praise him when he accepts the exchange.

In real life, you would be most likely to use this command when the dog has gotten into something truly heady like a deer carcass, so your established reward needs to be very powerful. A normal Bulldog won't trade a rotting carcass for a dry dog biscuit. Of course, you probably won't have any bacon actually on hand when the infraction occurs, but it's okay to cheat that one time. Afterward, practice "leave it" several more times with your accustomed treat and plenty of praise.

Sit

To teach your dog the sit, first grab a few pieces of tiny treats. Treats are absolutely essential. It's also important that you remember never to try to force your Bulldog to sit. Hold the treat *at your puppy's nose level*. Practice in a corner where he can't back up. As he extends his neck toward the treat, move your hand slowly over the top of his head (not too high) and back, saying, "Sit." Most dogs will automatically move into a sit in order to retrieve the treat. Give him the treat the instant he sits, and praise him enthusiastically. Practice several times, but keep the training session very short when puppies are involved. Five minutes is plenty of time for both you and your Bulldog.

Do not force your dog to complete this exercise; encourage him, and reward him with praise and a treat. Nothing about the training should be forced or painful. If your dog gets up too quickly, refrain from treating him. He needs to learn that the treat comes only when he is actually sitting. Otherwise, you'll turn him into a jack-in-the-box. You should have all of your family members perform this exercise until everyone knows the drill.

Teach your Bulldog to sit before he eats, before he goes out the door, or before any exciting activity. This will give him an

Basic Equipment

You can't train your dog without a few basic pieces of equipment. They include a buckle collar, leash, and treats. The need for additional equipment depends on what you're training your dog to do. If you are teaching your Bulldog to fetch, you'll need a ball. If you're teaching him to jump through a hoop, you'll need a hoop. The most important piece of equipment, though, is a good attitude on your part. This includes patience and a positive but realistic attitude about what you expect your Bulldog to do.

opportunity to calm down, and it will give you an opportunity to keep in control (and go out first).

Down

This is the next logical command after the sit. Most dogs rather dislike being asked to lie down, although they are happy enough to do it on their own. This is because the down puts them in a vulnerable position, both physically and psychologically.

To teach the down, use the treat method again. While the dog is sitting, lower the treat slowly and move it between his front legs toward the floor. Most dogs will lie down naturally. If yours doesn't after a few tries, you can gently extend his front legs and praise him as you ease him to the floor. Practice a few times before moving on to something else. Don't try to force him down. You want your dog to perform joyfully, not out of fear or pain.

In formal obedience classes, your Bulldog may learn a long down-stay, which usually lasts for several minutes. This command is simply a combination of down and stay. Bulldogs can be pretty good at this. Sometimes they even fall asleep!

Teach stay by saying the word and then slowly retreating.

Stay

Although some people teach the stay as a separate command, I prefer to use the sit, which means that my dog should sit until I say, "Okay!" I believe that teaching the stay as a separate command is confusing to dogs, because you're not asking them to do anything new—you're just asking them to keep doing what you have already asked them to do. However, other people believe that saying, "Stay" signals to the dog early that he'll be sitting for quite some time. At any rate, never ask your dog to sit-stay for more than a few seconds when you are starting out. You want to make success easy for him.

Teach stay by saying the word and gradually and slowly retreating. Reward him for remaining in one place.

Again, quit while the training is still fun. The length of time you teach this command depends on your individual dog, but five minutes is usually long enough.

Stand

The stand is a very important command for dogs to learn. After all, dogs stand while they are being bathed, groomed, and examined by the vet. Show dogs stand in the show ring. To teach this command, get out your trusty "lure" or "bait." Slowly raise the treat to where his nose would be if he were standing. Very soon he will "stand." At first you may have to hold him up and keep the treat a few inches in front of his nose so that he stretches to get it, but then he will soon catch on that he can stand and nibble the treat while it is still in your hand.

Come Tip

You want your Bulldog to associate the come command with pleasant things. Never use come to call your dog for anything unpleasant, like baths, trips to the vet, or medication.

Come

Although teaching your Bulldog to respond to your command to come is the most important lesson of all, sometimes it can be very difficult. Bulldogs, while anxious to please, are rather adamant about having their own way. As a result, the best plan is to make your wishes and your Bulldog's wishes one and the same. You must make him realize that you are the source of the treats, the pets, the praise, and the fun.

Never call your Bulldog for anything unpleasant, such as punishment, baths, or medication. When you have to give your dog a pill, you'll need to go after him yourself.

To encourage your Bulldog to come, you must make yourself the most enchanting object there is. Start indoors in a small room when your dog is young and most dependent upon you. Call him gently and offer a treat. Chances are he'll toddle over. Praise him with every step. If he doesn't come, gently draw the leash toward you while still encouraging him. Don't jerk on it. The purpose of the leash is to help him focus. You don't want your Bulldog to get the idea that it's even thinkable to go in a different direction than the one you're calling him to. When he responds by taking some steps in the right direction, praise him. When he reaches you, treat him. If he seems reluctant, try kneeling down so you are at the same level. This gives him confidence. Lean back and open your arms as you call him. This is an inviting gesture that usually elicits a positive response.

The leash is not merely a restraining device; rather, it is a way for you to stay close to your dog and keep him safe.

When you first begin teaching your Bulldog to come outdoors, use a short leash and have a treat available. Work the same way you did indoors. When he seems to understand, start working with a long leash. Use a 6-foot (2m) cotton lead, not a flexi-leash. Move away from him and encourage him to follow by calling softly to him. Dogs can see a moving target more clearly than one that is standing completely still. Chances are he'll follow you. Just in case, however, keep the leash attached to him for all of the early lessons. Never chase your dog, not even in play. You can't catch him, and it only encourages him to run faster.

Practice come three or four times a day. When your Bulldog becomes really good at it (at least two weeks of perfect behavior), experiment off lead in a secure area. Don't practice (yet) in times of high excitement or lots of distractions. He won't be able to concentrate, and that will guarantee a failure. Basically, you need to be more interesting to your dog than anything else.

Heel (Walk by Your Side)

Your Bulldog should be responding to the come command before you start teaching him to heel, which means to walk nicely on a lead at your heel. Your leash is your dog's best friend. Don't think of the leash as a restraining device; think of it as a way to stay close to your dog. Soon your Bulldog will look forward to the sight of the leash because it means it's time for a walk! However, Bulldogs are very strong dogs, and they can be pullers. Thus, it is doubly important for your dog to learn to walk calmly and pleasantly on a leash with you in control. If you don't teach your dog proper leash behavior very early, you're in for a difficult time.

When teaching your Bulldog to heel, don't pull or jerk on the leash. Only use it to keep him from going in the other direction. If your Bulldog starts to pull, turn the other way without a word. Keep repeating this exercise. This will focus his attention on you. Because no one likes to be pulled, he'll start paying attention and trying to anticipate your moves. Say, "Heel" in a quiet, firm voice as you turn. Don't go around aimlessly turning, however, just in order to confuse your dog. Turn only in response to his pulling against you. (When your dog becomes more adept at heeling, you can practice more complicated patterns.)

It is customary to have the dog walk on your left side when heeling. It doesn't really matter, but if you plan to engage in formal obedience training, you might as well start practicing correctly right away. Start by keeping a little treat in your left hand. The point is to get the dog to understand that staying close is likely to yield rewards.

PROBLEM BEHAVIORS

Even the extremely polite Bulldog can run into a few obstacles along his road to perfect behavior. Remember, though, that problem behaviors are problems for you, not the dog. What you see as a problem behavior, the dog sees as a solution. For example, let's say the dog tears the house up. For you, that's a problem. For the dog, it's a solution to his problem, which may be boredom or separation anxiety. You simply may not have seen your dog's boredom as a problem until he tried to do something about it. Oftentimes a truly destructive dog is responding to a problem in his life.

Treats can motivate your Bulldog in a positive way.

Basically, there are two approaches to problem behaviors, whether they exist in dogs or in people. The first approach is skilled therapy (or training), and the second is medication. While training can be effective by itself, medication is best used in conjunction with training.

Finding a Trainer

The Association of Pet Dog Trainers (APDT) can help you find a trainer in your area go to www.apdt.com for more information.

One of the most important questions you can ask yourself when you're dealing with a dog with a behavior problem is, "If I were my dog, how would I describe my owner?" The answer may tell you more than you think! The following are some descriptions of problem behaviors and some potential solutions. Consult a behavior specialist if you feel a particular behavior is too dangerous or difficult for you to handle.

Aggression

If your dog has growled, snarled, snapped, or bitten you when you tried to move him off the couch or take a toy away from him, he is being aggressive. If he growls or snaps at the vet, pet sitter, or groomer, he is being aggressive. Don't overlook or excuse this behavior. Some aggressive behavior is genetically linked, but other causes can include mishandling or various illnesses, like hypothyroidism or any disease in which pain makes him grouchy. If you feel the situation is out of hand, consult a trained behaviorist. Most pet dog trainers are not specifically trained in dealing with aggressive dogs, so talk to your veterinarian about finding certified help. The wrong treatment could make your dog worse, not better. A small percentage of dogs are beyond cure, but most are not.

Simply put, owners let aggression happen. They allow a dominant dog to take over the household. I have known people whose Bulldogs would not surrender their place on the sofa to humans, who snatched food fearlessly from human hands, who nipped children to get them out of the way, and who defended their food bowls with growls or snaps to keep human beings from coming too near. None of these are acceptable behaviors, although they're certainly natural enough.

"Natural" and "well-behaved" are not synonymous terms. A well-behaved Bulldog should:
- Move when asked.
- Give up his toys.
- Allow any human to approach his food bowl and pet him while he eats. (While you should allow a dog to eat in peace, a child is almost bound to break the rule, and you don't want an incident.)
- Keep all feet on the floor and jaws out of the way when humans are eating.
- Not nip unless provoked beyond bearing.

- Allow himself to be picked up and carried to the tub.
- Allow his nails to be clipped and his ears to be cleaned without undue complaint.

The basic rule is that all humans should be their dogs' leaders, and if your dog doesn't understand this rule, it's because you never taught it to him.

You must establish early that you are boss over your Bulldog. This doesn't mean you have to be harsh. In fact, Bulldogs don't respond well to harshness. Firmness, however, is a quality they admire. In fact, your dog is on the lookout for a good leader! You can be that leader, but you must prove yourself worthy by your firm, consistent training methods, your even temper, and your take-no-nonsense attitude. As leader, it's your job to decide when and where the dog eats, plays, and sleeps.

One particular arena in the battle for leadership occurs over furniture. To a bossy Bulldog, furniture is not merely a comfy place to sit. It's a fortress, a high place that allows him more status than does the lowly floor. Some dogs equate being high up with being in charge, so if your Bulldog tends toward bossiness, don't allow him couch privileges until he is ready to relinquish them to any human being (including a child) without an argument.

Whenever you are dealing with an overly assertive dog, stand up tall and speak in a firm, no-nonsense voice. If your Bulldog growls, snarls, or snaps at a person who tries to remove him from his roost, for example, you must take stern measures. Encourage his leave-taking with a firm "Off!" Don't make a big deal of it, but be firm. You may use food to lure your dog off the couch if he has not growled or snapped, but using food as a lure to a growler will seem like a reward to him for his behavior. Food is a great motivator for Bulldogs.

Don't allow a dominant dog on the couch or bed again. It's not usually hard to keep a Bulldog off, because they are not great jumpers. In fact, people usually have to help them on and then complain when there is a problem.

Possession Aggression

This unacceptable behavior pattern begins in puppyhood. In fact, it's unlikely that a dog who has

never shown aggressiveness over food or toys will suddenly begin doing so as an adult. Dogs demonstrating this behavior pattern will stand over their toy or food bowl and stare hard at anyone who approaches. In cases of food aggression, they will stop eating. The staring may be accompanied by growls, snapping, or biting. Obviously, this is something you'll need to nip in the bud.

First, you must realize that such behavior is actually quite natural. Dogs naturally wish to hang on to favored items, and in the wild, they know that if they give up their bone to another animal, they won't eat that day. However, even in the wild, dogs will surrender a meal to the dominant member of the pack. In your household, that's you. This is the way it should be in your home: You and all other human beings are the "top dog." Dogs aren't born seeing it that way, though; it's something they need to be taught. However, you don't teach them by snatching their food or toys away. That only confirms their suspicion that you are not their friend.

In order for dogs to overcome possession aggression, they first need to realize that they are in no danger of having their food permanently removed. When approaching a dog who seems to be guarding a treat, dog bowl, or toy, try trading that desirable item for an even more desirable item with him. For example, if he's eating kibble, he'll be happy to come over for a piece of cheese. In more serious cases, you may have to avoid giving him long-lasting chewing treats altogether, at least for a while. Give him only small biscuits he can devour at once without "owning" them. And in established cases of food aggression, it's wise to start by taking away your dog's food bowl completely and feeding him by hand until he becomes used to the basic idea that all food comes from you. If your dog seems suspicious of your approach, drop a tender morsel of food in the bowl every time he eats.

In less serious cases, it helps to keep the food bowl in a big, empty space rather than in a corner that's easier to protect. Don't give the dog his "special corner" in which to eat, either. Instead, move the bowl around and remove it immediately after the dog has eaten. Stay in the room while your Bulldog eats. This reinforces the idea that you still have control over his food. In addition, teach your Bulldog to sit and wait before you place his food bowl before him. If possible, teach him to wait until you give him permission to eat. Reward him for obeying by feeding him something better than what is in the bowl. (Let him know you have it first, or he'll wolf down the entire meal before you dig the piece of cheese out of your pocket.)

Some dogs take to "guarding" their owners, growling or snapping at the approach of other dogs or people. While most flattered owners assume the dog is protecting them, think again. What he's actually doing is guarding you—treating you like a favorite piece of rawhide. Don't be flattered. The dog is telling everyone, including you, that he owns you. If your dog guards you inappropriately, you will need to go back to the basics in establishing your leadership over him. Even if you want your Bulldog to guard you, that behavior should come on your initiative, not his.

Did You Know?

An enormous percentage of dog "problems" are caused by simple boredom on the part of the dog and can be solved merely by giving him more exercise, more interaction, and more attention. Before you decide your dog has a real problem behavior, try exercising him and spending more quality time with him.

Biting

Every year American insurance companies shell out about one billion dollars in settlements and lawsuits over biting dogs. As a rule, Bulldogs are gentle, but it's never safe to assume that your dog won't bite. Any dog, given the right (or wrong!) circumstances, will bite.

If your Bulldog has ever bitten anyone, especially for what appears to be no reason, take him to your vet for a thorough physical workup, especially if the behavior is new or sudden. It's possible he has a physical ailment. For example, he may have developed cataracts or another condition that limits his vision. This could lead to misidentification of a person or a general insecurity that could produce biting. Hypothyroidism, which is common in dogs, can lead to aggression. Chronic pain, like back or spinal problems, can also lead to aggressive behavior.

If your Bulldog is pronounced healthy, make an immediate appointment with a qualified animal behaviorist, not just any dog trainer. Most dog trainers do not have the specific background necessary to deal with aggression and can even make the problem worse by putting more pressure on the dog. Take careful notes of the circumstances under which the dog bit. Many cases of biting are limited to the biting of children or other members of the family whom the dog considers weak and of a lesser status. Most dog bites, in fact, involve family members or other people well known to the dog. This is called owner-directed aggression, and it doesn't typically come from so-called dominant dogs but from dogs who are stressed and anxious. They bite because they see biting as a sensible way to resolve conflict and keep people away.

These types of dogs bite because they have been allowed to believe that biting carries no negative consequences. The average biting dog is an unneutered male dog, poorly socialized, and in his early adolescence. His first victim is probably a young child. His next one might be you.

Handling Canine Aggression

When attempting to handle canine aggression, it's important to keep the following things in mind:

- Never provoke a situation where the dog may bite. Don't chase him, and don't attempt to pull him out of a hiding place. You're just asking for trouble
- Get your dog vet-checked for any possible physical problems.
- Enroll your dog in special obedience classes for aggressive dogs. Regular obedience classes may make a dog more anxious.
- For at least two weeks, keep your interactions with your dog down to a bare minimum; make him beg for your attention.
- Do not allow your dog on furniture, including the bed.
- Make the dog sit or lie down before feeding him.
- Give your dog twice the exercise he's getting now—outside in the yard. Working dogs are less stressed and much happier, meaning they are less apt to bite.
- If necessary, keep a soft muzzle on the dog while working with him.
- Keep small children completely away from the aggressive dog at all times unless the dog is muzzled.
- Consult your vet about possible anti-depressant medication
- Use a head halter rather than a conventional or choke collar if you can get one to fit.

Most dogs who bite have preceded the attack with a whole bunch of warning signs, most of which were covered up or ignored. He was probably allowed to mouth and chew on human fingers when he was puppy. He may have grabbed at a child's clothes or ankles as the child ran away. He may have grabbed food out of someone's hand, or he may have growled and refused to relinquish his place on the sofa to a person. He may have snapped when someone leaned over him. It should come as no surprise whatsoever when he finally bites someone. Most people think that aggressive dogs have been abused at some point in their lives. Actually, this is not true. Most aggressive dogs have been treated with kid gloves. Most families of biting dogs are quiet, gentle people. They are truly shocked when their beloved pet shows some trace of wolf-like behavior. They are afraid and heartbroken.

Fortunately, most of these stories can have a happy ending if the dog undergoes behavior therapy. Behavior therapy, sometimes combined with medications like tranquilizers and antidepressants, is usually effective in curing dog aggression as long as everyone in the family cooperates to help the dog. Most of these cases develop in the first place because the owners made errors in training their dog.

Never make excuses for a dog who bites. Telling yourself or others that he didn't mean to do it or blaming others for provoking him is putting your head in the sand. Biting is a very serious problem that can cause you to lose a lawsuit or your dog if you don't get it under control. Seek help.

Barking

Excessive barking is not a major problem in most Bulldogs, but there are exceptions. The key to handling the problem is to figure out why the dog is barking in the first place. Bulldogs usually bark to alarm their families of approaching visitors. While this is a valuable contribution to family security, praising this behavior too much can result in the Bulldog barking at every passing leaf in hopes of gaining the same attention. The secret is simply to say, "Thanks," and reward him after he has stopped barking.

Never yell at a barking dog. If you do, you're giving him attention, and dogs always bark to get some kind of attention— whether to alert you to a stranger or to call attention to his own neglected (in his eyes) state. Even negative attention like screaming

If your Bulldog tends to dig up your favorite flowers, solve the problem by giving him his own special place to dig.

at him is attention, and that's what he wants. If he's an indoor barker, ask him to sit after he has barked a few times to warn you of intruders. Then give him a treat. Dogs can't eat and bark at the same time. As I said earlier, though, barking is not a major problem with this breed.

Digging

A few Bulldogs have the unfortunate tendency to dig large, unsightly holes in the yard. However, digging a soft bed in the earth is a good way to keep cool, something that is very important to the Bulldog. Because dogs generally prefer digging in a soft spot, you might solve the problem by making your Bulldog his own earth box in a spot you have selected for him. Start him off by partially burying some favored toys in the dirt. With any luck, he may take the hint. For best results, place the box in a spot that gets afternoon shade. If your Bulldog's favorite digging place is your petunia bed, you may have to consider enclosing it so that he may gaze in admiration but not destroy it.

It's also a very good idea to provide your Bulldog with a child's wading pool in the summer, as long as he is carefully supervised. Get one made of heavy-duty plastic, and keep it filled with cool water. At night, use the contents of the pool to water your garden. (Leaving water standing around all night breeds mosquitoes.)

Do not punish your Bulldog for digging. He won't understand why you're doing it. Give him an alternate activity and manage the problem by supervision and attention instead.

Mouthing

Puppy mouthing is a natural but annoying practice. Puppy teeth are extremely sharp, partly to compensate for the lack of jaw power and partly to ensure the weaning process. To get your puppy to stop biting you, you need to let him know that it's inconvenient.

When he bites down, cry, "Ow!" in a yelping voice, and look (or move) away. He'll soon get the idea that when he bites hard, you won't play with him. This is one way to help your puppy develop what is called bite inhibition, an especially important skill for a Bulldog, who can bite down really, really hard. That's not something you want to experience!

Pulling

Powerful dogs like Bulldogs can be strong pullers. You can handle the problem with a no-pull harness, such as the Wayne Hightower harness, but it's also a good idea to train your dog to stop this annoying habit.

The first step is for you to control yourself. Getting out the leash is an exciting moment, and your dog is already in "pull mode" before it is snapped on. To help him control his enthusiasm, keep calm and collected yourself. It's a good idea to practice this training for the first time *after* a walk so that you have some chance of success.

Make your Bulldog sit and stay before you attach the leash. Do not walk out the door while he is jumping around in a frenzy. He will calm down only when he realizes that calm behavior will open the door, so until he settles down, do not open the door. Let him bounce around all he wants, but don't let him walk. When he settles down, praise him. Then, take a step with him on the leash away from the door. (The door is too exciting.) If he starts jumping around, stop again. Only head for the door when he is under control. Use the same method outside. When your Bulldog pulls, stop walking. If you continue to walk, he will understand that pulling has no consequences. You can also ask him to sit for a few seconds every time he starts to pull. (Obviously, the dog needs to know how to sit first.) Soon you will have a reliable walker at your side.

Chewing

Destructive chewing is both annoying and dangerous. Powerful Bulldog jaws can turn your furniture into matchsticks and your carpet into shreds. Bulldogs can devour linoleum and bend forks. They can even chew through cans.

All dogs need to chew, so this is not a behavior we can eliminate. It is, however, a behavior we need to channel. To do this, first make sure your Bulldog has a number of safe toys to chew. If

Did You Know?

One common misbehavior you will seldom see in Bulldogs is jumping up. Bulldogs like to keep all four legs on the floor. When you do have a Bulldog who jumps, simply don't give him the reward he is looking for—attention from you. Turn your back and walk away. He will soon stop.

Nylabone®

he has appropriate toys but still prefers to wreak havoc on furniture, then he must be crated.

Much destructive chewing has nothing to do with the normal need to chew. It's a result of boredom or despair. In these cases, the way to stop chewing is to put an end to your dog's boredom. If your Bulldog gets a sufficient amount of exercise and attention, most of his chewing problems will cease.

Food Stealing

Bulldogs are quite attracted to food. After all, it's only natural, and like all mammals they are programmed to be hungry at all times. Dogs do not have an evolved moral sense that tells them stealing is wrong. They are opportunists! The first step in putting a stop to this behavior is to manage the situation yourself. Don't leave food around if you can help it. Very few dogs have the self-control not to eat a cookie when it is dropped right in front of them. Controlling this behavior is more a matter of training yourself to keep your food where it belongs than training the dog.

Noise Phobia

A phobia is defined as an excessive, irrational fear response. Dogs can have them, just as people do, and they can occur in any breed at any age. However, a phobia generally manifests itself first in dogs between the ages of six months and a year. Phobias tend to become more severe as dogs age.

Sometimes a phobia will develop gradually over time, while other times it can emerge after one single scary encounter. Unfortunately, without intervention, the dog may become more afraid with each exposure to the provocation. The phobia can spread to other things as well. A dog may begin by being afraid of thunder, but his phobia may take over to the point where he fears accompanying rain, too, and eventually becomes afraid of rain, even when there is no thunder at all. Whatever the trigger, there seems to be a genetic basis for it.

Noise-phobic dogs may salivate, hide, pace, whine, or pant. Some can even injure themselves in their attempt to escape. They may hide in the bathroom or another cool, dark room. Interestingly enough, dogs prefer humid rooms to hide in, and some people suspect that this has to do with the static electricity associated with thunderstorms.

Thunder Phobia

About 19 percent of dogs have thunder phobia. Dogs may be clued in to approaching thunder by the change in barometric pressure. Dogs appear very sensitive to this, and many appear to find it disturbing. Some dogs simply elect to tear the house apart. Although phobic dogs do tend to hide during a thunderstorm, it doesn't do any good to attempt to lock them up in a crate. This will just increase their anxiety.

While even the most intelligent dog may fear thunder and fireworks, he may not be able to avoid either of them. In mild cases, you can simply turn on the radio, television, or air conditioner—anything to supply a kind of white noise to cover the offending sound.

More serious cases may require sterner measures. While various kinds of psychoactive drugs have been tried on noise-phobic dogs, current research suggests that the best approach to curing your dog of this fear is a two-pronged approach that includes audio recording desensitization and dog-appeasing pheromones (DAPs). Another solution is melatonin. This natural, over-the-counter hormone is produced by the pineal gland and has a remarkable effect on the thunderstruck. You can buy melatonin in health food stores. Other veterinarians have reported success with a combination of clomipramine and alprazolam. However, you must discuss these options with your veterinarian. What doesn't work is coddling your Bulldog and telling him not to worry. Your very tone will convince him that he has reason to be concerned.

Separation Anxiety

One of the most serious psychological disorders of the contemporary dog is separation anxiety. Technically, it's not even a disorder; it's simply a dog's way of solving a terrible dilemma, like being alone, scared, or bored.

Dogs have been bred and conditioned for millennia to thrive on human company. When that company is missing, some dogs find the pain of separation intolerable. Our canine companions just weren't designed to spend hour after hour alone. Dogs who have suffered abandonment in the past are especially prone to separation anxiety. They have no way of knowing if or when you'll return after you shut that door. This has to be a frightening experience.

People who have dogs who suffer from separation anxiety return home to find shredded sofas, chomped up chairs, ravaged rugs, and a shaking, cowering, or manic dog. And once it starts, it tends to get worse, partly because the owner begins to regard the impending separation with equal fear, although for different reasons—the dread of what she will find when returning home! The dog picks up the owner's tension, and he in turn becomes even more stressed, leading to more destruction, defecation, and despair.

Play Biting

Small puppies can gently mouth your hand without a problem, but by the time the dog is 12 to 16 weeks old, he can be rough. Discourage him from getting carried away. If he bites your hand in play too hard, yip fearfully and leave him to his own devices. He'll soon learn that hard nipping results in the loss of a playmate.

If he starts chewing on an inappropriate object, immediately trade with him for something better and praise him when he actually plays with it or chews it.

Treatment for this serious problem includes a course of therapy that combines careful counterconditioning with appropriate medication. For best results, both should be used together. The behavioral aspect of the therapy is the most difficult, and it should only be undertaken with the help of a certified animal behaviorist, preferably one who is also a veterinarian and can prescribe the medication in appropriate doses

To keep both your home and your Bulldog safe, you may need to confine a destructive dog in your absence. Don't use a crate if you'll be gone long, however. A crated dog simply doesn't have enough to do, and the barrier stress could really bother him. Instead, put him in a large room with a rotating variety of chew toys, a comfortable, inviting bed, and access to water.

To accustom your dog to your absences, practice taking short (just a minute or so) trips at first. Practice getting ready to leave (jingling keys, putting on your coat, even jiggling the door), but don't actually leave. The dog has associated your jingling keys, the act of putting on your coat, and jiggling the door with you leaving. Try dissociating these activities with leaving, and your actual departure may be less stressful for him. In other words, try to defuse the situation by not providing the dog with the accustomed cues you have been giving him as you exit the house.

When you do leave, just go. Don't hang around the house wringing your hands or attempting to comfort the dog with kisses. He'll just feel worse when you finally withdraw. The more you're able to ignore him in the minutes before you leave, the easier the separation will be on him. While you're gone, provide him with a distracting toy, a special something he gets only when you leave. Most dogs enjoy something that contains food. Many items are on the market that have places to stash a few treats, and your dog can spend quite a while figuring out how to remove them. This displaces his anxiety and he may feel much better all day. Leave the television or radio on also. It's comforting to many dogs.

Establishing yourself as a trusted leader is very helpful for dogs with separation anxiety. As the bond between you strengthens, the dog will begin to have faith that you are making the right decisions. If you abdicate your leadership role, your Bulldog will think that he's in charge, and he doesn't really know how to do that. This will lead to more anxiety and more destruction. Be the leader you were born to be and your dog can relax.

In serious cases, you may need to resort to a trained behaviorist and a medical solution.

MEDICATION

As mentioned earlier, when dealing with serious problem behaviors, medication in conjunction with behavior modification may be the best solution.

Veterinary behaviorists use many of the same kinds of drugs with dogs as physicians use with people. That's because dogs suffer the same types of problems, including phobias, aggression, anxiety, compulsive disorders, hyperactivity, and even self-mutilation. Most psychoactive drugs act by regulating neurotransmitters like serotonin, dopamine, and norepinephrine, which act between the junctions of brain cells. Psychoactive drugs, called Selective Serotonin Reuptake Inhibitors (SSRIs), increase the amount of serotonin available, which tends to stabilize mood and decrease owner-directed aggression. Other drugs can help with separation anxiety, while still others work wonders for senior dogs with canine cognitive dysfunction. However, most of these drugs

To help a Bulldog with separation anxiety, give him a variety of chew toys to play with in your absence.

are not meant to be used alone, but in combination with behavioral training and therapy. Recently, behaviorists have had success with pheromones, particularly DAPs (dog-appeasing pheromones) that have a reassuring effect on dogs. They have no side effects, either, which is a great first step.

No one training method or medication is a surefire "magic bullet" for all dogs. Every dog is a complex individual who responds differently to a variety of stimuli, just like people. Don't be afraid to experiment with different approaches to get the result you want: a controllable, happy, responsive pet. Your Bulldog is depending on you to make that happen.

ADVANCED TRAINING and ACTIVITIES

With Your Bulldog

Bulldogs are eligible to participate in many activities, but because of their peculiar anatomy, not to mention interesting character, not all are equally feasible. You know your Bulldog best, but if lure coursing or sheep herding is your dream, your Bulldog can turn it into a nightmare. Fortunately, the Bulldog is one of the world's best companion dogs, and no one need ask for more. At the same time, there are a few things your Bulldog might be interested in, and you should certainly try them out!

Your Bulldog should already know how to sit, lie down, and stay at this point, so what's next? If you're ambitious, all kinds of activities await you and Bulldog. However, before you jump into a new activity, there are a few things you need to keep in mind:

- Research the activity. Figure out if you have the time, money, energy, or even a real interest in whatever activity you're considering.
- Make sure your Bulldog undergoes a thorough veterinary checkup. You not only don't want to work a sick dog, but you want to know what your Bulldog's general health is before you embark on an exercise program.
- Start slowly. Even if your Bulldog gets a clean bill of health, go slow, just as a human athlete would. Don't stress your dog beyond his natural limits.
- If your dog will be doing endurance work, beef up his fat and protein intake.
- Quit when you've had enough. Remember, you are both supposed to be having *fun*!

CANINE GOOD CITIZEN® PROGRAM

The Canine Good Citizen® (CGC) test is your first step toward formal recognition for your wonderful, socialized, well-trained Bulldog. Spayed and neutered dogs are welcome. Begun in 1989, Canine Good Citizen® is a certification program created and administered by the American Kennel Club to reward dogs who show good manners in their community. It not only lays the basic foundation for more advanced work in performance events, but it also gives your pet the basic skills he needs to negotiate life successfully.

The Canine Good Citizen® test is open to all dogs, whether mixed breed or purebred, and there is no age limit, although the dog must be old enough to have received his immunizations. You will need a leash and collar (buckle or slip-type collar; no special training collars, such as a prong collar or head halter, are permitted) and a brush/comb for grooming. Your dog should be well groomed and in healthy condition.

The test consists of ten steps, and dogs who pass it will receive a very nice certificate from the American Kennel Club. This is a great opportunity to educate, bond with, and have fun with your dog. You'll both benefit!

DOG SHOWS (CONFORMATION)

Dog Shows in the United States

In the United States, the dog show is the glamour contest for dogs; they are the ones you see prancing around Madison Square

A show dog must be taught how to stack and stand still while being examined.

The Kennel Club's Good Citizen Dog Scheme

In 1992, the Kennel Club launched a new training program called the Good Citizen Dog Scheme to promote responsible dog ownership in the UK. Since then, over 52,000 dogs have passed the test, which is administered through 1,050 training organizations.

Any dog is eligible to take part in the Good Citizen Dog Scheme, a noncompetitive plan that trains owners and dogs for everyday situations and grants four awards—bronze, silver, gold, and puppy foundation assessment—based on the level of training that both dog and owner have reached together.

For more information, refer to the Kennel Club's website at www.the-kennel-club.org.uk.

Garden every February at the Westminster Kennel Club show or on other shows now aired on television.

Each year, the American Kennel Club alone hosts 15,000 competitive events of all kinds. Some dog shows are formal competitions for titles (the AKC offers about 40 different titles—something for everyone); others, often called "matches," are informal events. While there can only be one overall winner, the Best in Show, at any show there are lots and lots of ribbons to go around. I should reiterate, however, that you can't hope to do well at a dog show unless you own a show-quality Bulldog. As the rules now stand, only unneutered, unspayed dogs can be shown in most AKC conformation events.

If your dog is show quality, your knowledgeable breeder or a member of your local Bulldog club will tell you. Showing a dog, however, is not as easy as picking up a leash and running around the ring. Your dog needs to be taught to "stack" (pose properly), stand still while being examined, and "show his heart out." A winning dog has more than good conformation and a powerful way of moving. He has that indefinable "something" that says to the show judge, "Look at *me*! I'm the winner here!" Some absolutely drop-dead gorgeous dogs simply don't have the attitude it takes to get to the top levels.

For most people, that top level is an AKC Championship. To get there, your dog needs to earn 15 points under at least three different judges. (Obviously, this is to prevent you from following your dog show judge Uncle Lucius from show to show.) In

Local dog shows allow dogs to earn points toward their championship.

addition, your Bulldog must win at least two "majors" at larger shows, where he'll face more competition. How many Bulldogs it takes to make a "major" depends upon how many Bulldogs are registered in the area where the show is being held. A show may be a major for Pekinese but not for Bulldogs, or vice versa. You won't know if it's a major until a week or so before the show, and even then, if enough dogs are no-shows, the major is "broken." Points are awarded based on the number of dogs who actually show up to be judged. Every show is worth between one and five points, with a major being a show worth three points or more.

Male dogs compete against males and females against females in each breed, with the best of each sex awarded points toward his or her championship. The best animal of each breed is then named "Best of Breed" and competes against others in his group. In the case of the Bulldog, this is the Non-Sporting Group, which also includes American Eskimo Dogs, Lhasa Apsos, Dalmatians, and Schipperkes, among others. (This group is really kind of a mixed-bag group of dogs who don't seem to fit into any other group.) The winner of the Non-Sporting Group goes to Best in Show to compete against the other group winners.

A dog show is really a giant elimination contest. Westminster is only for champions, but the local dog shows held near you allow dogs to earn points toward their championship.

Even if you don't make it to Westminster, you can show your quality Bulldog at many dog shows nearly every weekend. This is a fun, family-oriented sport that is open to people of all ages!

Dog Shows in the United Kingdom

The most famous dog show in the United States is Westminster, but the United Kingdom can match it with Crufts. Crufts is somewhat more informal than Westminster. It is run by the Kennel Club and features 197 different breeds (more than are recognized in the United States). The original Cruft, Charles, made his living selling dog cakes all across Europe. Inspired by the wide variety of breeds, he organized the first show in 1891. Today in the United Kingdom, there are basically two kinds of shows: Open Shows, which are informal, even casual, and Champion shows, which are much more competitive.

As in the United States, the breeds are divided into groups, although the groupings are different from those the American Kennel Club uses. The Kennel Club recognizes hounds, gundogs, terriers, utility, working, pastoral, and toys. Bulldogs are in the Utility Group. In the United Kingdom, the Kennel Club is responsible for the licensing of nearly 5,000 canine competitions a year. These events are held under Kennel Club regulations and include breed shows, field trials, working trials, and obedience and agility competitions. Any dog registered with the Kennel Club is eligible to compete at these Kennel Club events.

Like the United States, the Kennel Club offers both multi-breed and single-breed conformation shows. Classes are also divided by the age of the dog (Minor puppy for 6- to 9-month-old dogs, Puppy for 6- to 12-month-old dogs, and Junior for dogs between 12 and 18 months of age). There are also divisions between Limited, Open, and Championship shows. For more information about the British show scene, visit www.the-kennel-club.org.uk.

Did You Know?

Next to the Kentucky Derby, the Westminster Kennel Club dog show is the oldest continuous sporting event held in the United States. Only dogs who have already attained a championship are allowed to compete. Top-ranked dogs across the country receive an invitation to compete.

FORMAL OBEDIENCE

Bulldogs are not known as obedience dogs. Although Bulldogs are highly intelligent animals who readily learn basic good manners, most do not shine at formal obedience. One reason for the comparative rarity of their achievements in obedience is that this event requires a dog to retrieve, and Bulldogs are not natural retrievers. They can be taught to go after a ball or stick, but getting them to bring it back is something else again. However, that doesn't mean they can't do it or that they are stupid. As a matter of fact, from 1930 to 2004, 543 Bulldogs have attained their CD (Companion Dog) title. That's about seven dogs every year. These aren't Labrador statistics, of course, but if you're working with Bulldogs, you have to take what you can get. The step beyond the CD title is CDX (Companion Dog Excellent). To date, about 84 Bulldogs have made it that far, a little more than one per year. Fifteen Bulldogs have progressed beyond that to UD, or Utility Dog. And only two Bulldogs have completed their UDX, Utility Dog Excellent. Their names (for they deserve recognition for their feats) are Beefeater's Amazin' Grace of SBK in 2001, owned by Laura Haney and Cheryl Knapp, and Sir Charles Barkley IX in 2004, owned by Betty Studzinki.

Today, obedience trials offered by the American Kennel Club are held in conjunction with most all-breed dog shows. Spayed and neutered dogs are welcome to participate. The great thing about obedience is that all of the dogs can return home as winners. Although some may score higher than others, obedience trials test your dog's ability to perform certain scored exercises. In each exercise, your dog must score more than 50 percent of the possible points (ranging from 20 to 40) and achieve a total score of at least 170 out of a possible 200. Each trial is a "leg" toward your dog's

Some Bulldogs enjoy tracking, a sport that involves a harness, long lead, and articles to be tracked, or sniffed out.

CD. You need three legs altogether.

Classes are divided to reflect the experience of the owners involved. So-called "A" classes are for beginners whose dogs have never received a title, while "B" classes are for more experienced handlers. After your dog wins his CD, he's eligible to continue toward more advanced titles like CDX, UD, or UDX. To attain these, your dog needs three "legs" in each as well.

To achieve a CD, a dog must heel on leash, heel free, stand for examination, recall, and complete a long sit (60 seconds) and a long down (three minutes). When heeling, he'll have to execute left and right turns, stops, and move at various speeds. On the "stand," he'll need to stand still off lead while a judge examines him. The handler must be at least 6 feet away. The recall requires the dog to sit 30 feet from the handler, come quickly, and then sit. On command, the dog will move to the heel position and sit once more. At the CDX and UD level, the dogs must work entirely off lead and show a higher level of skill. The best way to get started in obedience is to join your local kennel club.

In the United Kingdom, you can enter Pre-Beginner, Beginner, Novice, Open, A, B, and Championship C Classes. Exercises include scent discrimination, where your dog is expected to retrieve a particular article from a selection laid out in the ring; distance control, when your dog must obey commands to sit, stand, or down, given while you are standing some distance away from him; and heel work at different speeds and with many different maneuvers.

What is Agility?

Agility is a competitive sport in which dogs maneuver through a timed obstacle course. The course can contain obstacles such as tunnels, jumps, weave poles, and teeter-totters.

AGILITY

All breeds are involved in AKC agility; five jump heights are provided for all sorts of leg lengths. A standard agility course has 20 obstacles spread over about 180 yards. Most competitive dogs, guided by their handlers, cover such distances in 50 seconds or less. A Bulldog might take 50 days. Only ten agility titles were handed out to Bulldogs in 2003, so it isn't an easy accomplishment. While it is possible, many Bulldogs lack the stamina to handle an agility course.

TRACKING

In tracking, your dog will wear a special harness that allows free range of movement. You also need a 20 to 40 foot lead and some "articles," such as a wallet or a pair of leather gloves. Both the American Kennel Club and the United Kennel Club offer titles in this sport.

Bulldogs face the same kinds of difficulties when participating in tracking events that they do in obedience training. They are not natural scent hounds, and although they are quite good at finding things, they prefer to look for them rather than smell the ground. (In that respect, as in so many others, they are like us.) Since tracking dogs are expected to follow a scent on the ground, Bulldogs are at a disadvantage.

OTHER SPORTING EVENTS

American Kennel Club rules do not permit Bulldogs to compete in earth trials, lure coursing, or herding. That's a good thing, because Bulldogs are not interested in digging around after rodents, chasing plastic bags on a pulley, or herding anything.

EXERCISE AND GAMES

For the well-adjusted Bulldog, tug-of-war is a fun game that can be played in a small area.

If you have a playful Bulldog, it's a great temptation to get him to run around with you. You have to be careful, though. Not only are the Bulldog's infamous breathing problems a hindrance to

vigorous exercise, but too much exercise too early can be detrimental. This is true with many heavy breeds. Until your Bulldog is a year old, walking (not jumping) is the healthiest policy. However, this doesn't mean that you shouldn't give your dog adequate exercise! Bulldogs need it as much as any other dog. While you should give your dog a chance to develop strong bones and ligaments, you need to recognize his limits, even if he does not. The key is to exercise your dog without stressing him.

As a rule, Bulldogs are more like philosophers than athletes. While you may have one who enjoys fetch or tugging on a rope, it's not a given. Experiment with different activities to see what your particular dog enjoys!

Kennel Club Sporting Events

The Kennel Club in the United Kingdom sponsors a variety of events for Bulldogs and their owners to enjoy together. For complete listings, rules, and descriptions, please refer to the Kennel Club's website at www.the-kennel-club.org.uk.

Agility

Introduced in 1978 at Crufts, agility is a fun, fast-paced, and interactive sport. The event mainly consists of multiple obstacles on a timed course that a dog must handle. Different classes have varying levels of difficulty.

Flyball

Flyball is an exciting sport introduced at Crufts in 1990. Competition involves a relay race in which several teams compete against each other and the clock. Equipment includes hurdles, a flyball box, backstop board, and balls.

Obedience

Obedience competitions test owner and dog's ability to work together as a team. There are three types of obedience tests, which include the Limited Obedience Show, Open Obedience Show, and Championship Obedience Show. Competition becomes successively more difficult with each type of show.

Walking and Jogging

Don't expect to get a lot of exercise yourself while walking a Bulldog. They don't go very fast (for a dog), and they like to take their time to examine their surroundings. Allow them this pleasure, and take some time to enjoy the surroundings yourself. You can always jog later. At the same time, I can't overemphasize the importance of allowing your Bulldog to move at his own pace. These animals are very susceptible to heatstroke, as I discuss in Chapter 8. If you desire a jogging companion, another breed is a better choice.

Participating in activities, like fetch, is a great way to exercise your Bulldog.

Fetch

Bulldogs can fetch, but many would prefer not to. In many instances, a Bulldog is quite anxious to get the ball but not particularly interested in giving it back. In that case, the dog has taken charge of the game. To regain control, throw the toy, and when your Bulldog has picked it up, run in the opposite direction. When he gets close enough, take the toy by trading it for a treat. Try this method a few more times.

Some Bulldogs are simply not interested in chasing a ball or toy at all. If this is the case with your dog, try something else, like tug-of-war.

Tug-of-War

For a long time, people were told not to play tug with their dogs, as it made them aggressive and dominant. This is not true, although you probably should avoid this game with an animal who has had domination or aggression problems in the past. For the normal Bulldog, however, tug-of-war is a perfectly suitable game. It provides great exercise and can be played in a small area.

Select a simple tug toy like a tug rope that the dog will come to recognize as the cue for the game, and use it only for tug-of-war. Devise a special command to begin the game, like "Let's TUG!"

Your dog will naturally want to grab the tug rope. If he grabs the rope without permission, don't play—he should release it on command. If he does not do this, teach him by trading the rope for a treat. As soon as you get the rope from him, give it right back and praise him. This will make him more amenable to giving up his cherished rope. If he runs off with the toy, don't chase him. He'll soon return with it for more tugs.

You can also interrupt the game with a few obedience commands from time to time. This will sharpen his skills and keep him listening to you. Don't allow the dog to touch you with his teeth. If you receive a nip, stop the game immediately for at least five minutes. He'll get the picture.

THERAPY DOGS

Therapy dogs comfort the sick, cheer the elderly, and heal those who are suffering from emotional issues. They provide benefits for heart patients, AIDS patients, the disabled, and homeless children. They have even been used to help rehabilitate prisoners! Fortunately, the calm, friendly, and charming Bulldog makes the ideal therapy dog. They are sturdy enough not to be easily knocked over and small enough not to be clumsy or intimidating in hospitals and nursing homes. They are also soft and don't mind being petted.

To transform your Bulldog into a therapy dog, it's best to have your pet certified, either through the facility you'll be volunteering at or through a national pet therapy organization. In some cases, you'll just be making the rounds, visiting and talking with residents (many of whom have literally no one else to talk to). In other cases, your pet will be part of a specific treatment plan, with clear goals set forth on each visit.

Certification programs vary, but many require that your dog complete a full obedience course and a health screening and be of a certain age (usually one year). Of course, a good therapy dog should be bathed and groomed (especially the nails) and flea-free. As far as personality is concerned, two qualities are of the essence: friendliness and obedience. To find out what programs may be available in your area, contact a local nursing home or hospital. Two national organizations, Therapy Dogs International (www.tdi-dog.org) and the Delta Society (www.deltasociety.org), offer country-wide programs.

HEALTH

of Your Bulldog

Nothing is more important than your Bulldog's health. As his owner and guardian, you are largely responsible for maintaining it. The keys to health, which include the proper diet and exercise, preventive care, and clean surroundings, are in your hands!

VISITING THE VETERINARIAN

Your Bulldog's happiness depends largely on his health. To that end, a good relationship with a wise and compassionate veterinarian is essential. Next to you, your vet is your dog's best friend.

It's a good idea to secure a vet before you even bring your Bulldog home. Look for one you can trust who understands the special nature of Bulldogs.

Questions to Ask the Vet

If this is the first trip to the veterinarian for you and your Bulldog, check the place out—don't be afraid to ask for a tour. Also, consider the following questions when making this very important choice for you and your canine companion:

- Do staff members seem relaxed, friendly, and compassionate, or do they have a "this is just a business" aura?
- What services do they provide? Boarding? Grooming? Home visits?
- Are any of the staff specialists in orthopedics, holistic treatments, behavior, or cardiology?
  - What hours is the clinic open? Evenings? Weekends? Who answers the calls when the office is closed? (If you work days, you should choose a clinic with evening hours.)
  - How close is the vet to your home? A difference of five minutes can mean life or death for your Bulldog.

- Does the clinic accept pet insurance?
- Is the clinic a member of a spay/neuter program?
- How many Bulldogs does the clinic handle, and how familiar is the staff with the Bulldog's special health concerns?

One of the most important things to remember when researching veterinarians is that you need the help of a vet versed in Bulldogdom. Bulldogs are a peculiar breed with special health problems (especially respiratory), particularly when it comes to anesthesia. Many otherwise excellent vets are stymied when it comes to this breed. However, once you find a good vet, never let her go!

The First Visit

Make the first visit to the vet a fun one, with lots of treats, pets, and playtime. If all goes well, the first trip will be for a checkup only, so your dog won't have any painful associations with the visit. If you are calm and happy yourself, your mood will definitely rub off on your Bulldog. On the other hand, if you're tense and nervous, you'll convey these feelings to the dog.

Because your Bulldog's health is so important, finding a vet you trust is essential.

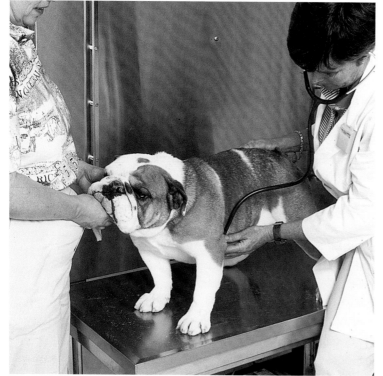

Make sure the first checkup takes place within 48 hours of getting your Bulldog, if possible, and bring along a stool sample so the veterinarian can check for worms, most of which are invisible to the naked eye. If he's not a show dog, you should also make a spay/neuter appointment. He'll live a longer, healthier, happier life, and you'll be doing your bit to reduce the problem of pet overpopulation. Of course, you should take your Bulldog to your vet for regular checkups as well.

The initial checkup will include a good look at your dog's teeth, eyes, and ears. Your vet will listen to his heart and lungs to detect heart murmurs, an irregular heartbeat, or harsh lung sounds. There will be a general inspection for lumps and bumps, dry skin, fleas, and ticks. Your Bulldog will also be weighed, and you'll probably receive a lecture on feeding and nutrition. The vet may test each limb and joint for range of motion, and she may poke your dog's stomach to check for pain or enlarged organs. The belly button will be examined for an umbilical hernia.

Owner Responsibilities

Of course, you have a responsibility for your Bulldog's health too! Good Bulldog owners know their part of the equation includes:

- Supplying a good diet
- Providing adequate exercise
- Keeping the dog up-to-date on vaccinations and regular health checkups
- Brushing the dog's teeth daily
- Grooming regularly and using that opportunity to check ears, eyes, teeth, and nails
- Observing the dog's habits and noting any changes
- Loving, cuddling, and interacting with the dog

I don't recommend buying vaccines online and then giving them yourself to save a few dollars. Vaccines need to be handled in a certain way and administered according to certain protocol. Let a medical professional do it and check your dog over at the same time. All vaccine brands are not the same quality, by the way. Do you know which is which? Your vet does.

VACCINATIONS

Vaccinations save lives. Before the days of effective veterinary vaccines, dogs were victims of canine distemper, hepatitis, and rabies. Now these diseases are rare. When parvo first emerged on the scene in the late 1970s, many dogs died before a vaccine was developed. While there is an ongoing discussion about how often and against what diseases your dog needs to be vaccinated, you owe it to your dog and your community to do your research and make an informed choice. Consult with your veterinarian to ask about his vaccine protocol, and don't be afraid to ask questions.

Vaccination Protocol

While vaccination scheduling is a matter of controversy (and is constantly changing), here are the current recommendations for most dogs.

Questions to Ask the Vet

Many times I get calls from people who say, "My vet diagnosed my dog with Carpiothyburoforkoliosis (or whatever). How bad is that? Should he be on a special diet? Is it catching?"

I always respond, "Well, I don't know. What did your vet say?"

They reply, "I didn't ask." Or, "He told me but I forgot." Or, "He told me but I didn't understand what he meant."

Don't be afraid to ask your veterinarian questions! Ensuring that you are well-informed will assist you in making the best choices for your beloved Bulldog. Here are some of the most important questions to ask if your dog has been diagnosed with a serious ailment:

- **"What does my dog have, exactly?"** Get both the official medical name for the disorder as well as a down-to-earth explanation of what it means.

- **"What's the prognosis?"** This means you're asking your vet to predict the final outcome of the disease. Is the disease curable? Treatable? If not, will it eventually kill your dog? These are hard questions, but you need to know.

- **"What's the best course of action, and how will it help my dog?"** Your vet may want to perform surgery or use radiation, herbs, or acupuncture, so you need to find out what he wants to do and how it will help.

- **"How will this disease and its treatment affect my dog?"** You'll want to know if your dog will be listless, lose his appetite, or experience problems with housetraining. If the disease is transmittable to your other dogs, you will want to know that also.

- **"What responsibility will I have for his care?"** Your dog's illness may require you to medicate him regularly or even take him for treatments elsewhere.

- **"Should my pet see a specialist?"** Veterinary medicine has as many specialists as human medicine does. You are not insulting your general practitioner vet if you ask to see an oncologist, ophthalmologist, or whatever specialist your dog may require.

- **"How much will this cost?"** This is a fair and legitimate question. Ask it.

- **"When should I check back if my dog is not improving as expected?"** You should be aware of the progress your dog is expected to make within a certain time period. This will help you determine when to further consult with your vet.

Finally, get everything in writing, and don't leave the office until you completely understand. If you get home and realize you forgot to ask something, call your vet back. If you are not satisfied with something and can't work it out, see a different vet. There's no profit in wandering about in ignorance or uncertainty, and your Bulldog will be the one who suffers.

Puppies 4 to 20 Weeks of Age

The vaccination series begins between six and eight weeks of age. Typically, the last vaccination is given between 14 and 16 weeks of age. These early vaccines should protect against canine distemper virus, canine adenovirus, parainfluenza, and canine parvovirus. In cases where your dog is exposed to others in a closed area, a vaccine against bordetella is recommended. The rabies vaccine should be given in accordance with individual state laws, usually between 16 and 26 weeks of age. Newer vaccines that are effective against specific forms of leptospirosis are given in certain affected areas. Check with your vet.

Dogs 20 Weeks to 2 Years of Age

Young adults need booster shots to ensure lifelong immunity against the same diseases they were vaccinated against as puppies.

Dogs Over 2 Years of Age

If your dog has had his puppy shots and boosters, you and your vet may wish to forgo further vaccination for three or four years. It is increasingly recognized that annual vaccinations are not necessary, although annual checkups certainly are!

Diseases to Protect Against

Although vaccination protocols differ from place to place and even from vet to vet, consider vaccinating your puppy against the following diseases.

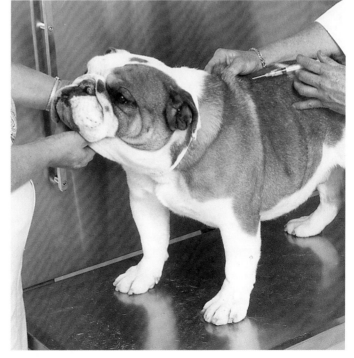

Young adults need booster shots to protect them from various diseases.

Parvovirus

Parvovirus is a highly contagious, deadly virus that first appeared in 1978. It is transmitted through the feces of infected dogs. This virus invades and destroys rapidly growing cells in the intestine, bone marrow, lymphoid tissue, and even the heart muscles, resulting in nausea, depression, vomiting, and severe bloody diarrhea. The disease can vary from mild to fatal, especially in puppies if they are not properly treated. To make matters worse, parvo is a cold-hardy virus, which means that it can survive in infected feces at temperatures as low as 4°F

(-15°C). The incubation period is from two to seven days.

Distemper

Distemper is the main killer of dogs worldwide. It destroys the nervous system and attacks every tissue in the body. It is caused by an airborne, measles-like virus. The incubation period is 7 to 21 days, and initial symptoms include lethargy, fever, runny nose, and yellow discharge from the eyes. The dog will demonstrate labored breathing, lose his appetite, and experience diarrhea and vomiting. Later symptoms include a nervous twitch, seizures, and thickening of the paw pads and nose, which is why the disease was once known as "hardpad." Dogs who progress to this stage are unlikely to make a complete recovery.

Hepatitis

Hepatitis is a serious disease caused by an adenovirus and is most dangerous in puppies. It is spread by contact with an infected dog or the infected dog's urine or feces. The white blood cell count drops, and some dogs experience clotting problems. It also affects the kidneys and liver. Symptoms include high fever, red mucous membranes, depression, and loss of appetite. Small blood spots may appear on the gums, and the eyes will look bluish. Even dogs who recover often experience chronic illnesses; they may also shed the virus for months, infecting others in the process. Luckily, this disease is seldom seen nowadays, largely because of the effective vaccines against it.

In some cases, your dog may require vaccinations against coronavirus, Lyme disease, and giardia. Ask your vet for her recommendations.

Leptospirosis

Leptospirosis is a worldwide bacterial infection that can be passed on to human beings. Dogs can contract this disease through exposure to the urine of an infected dog, rat, or wild animal. Leptospirosis affects the liver and kidneys, and in its most dangerous form can even shut the kidneys down. Even if the dog survives the disease, he can have permanent kidney damage. Treatment includes antibiotics, and in the case of kidney failure, dialysis. A vaccine is available for some forms of leptospirosis; however, many vets do not recommend its use, especially for young puppies. The "older" forms of leptospirosis are seldom seen nowadays, and the vaccine can cause reactions in some dogs. Recently, the disease has returned in a new and virulent strain, one that was previously seen only in horses and cows. A vaccine against this "new" lepto strain is being tested.

Rabies

Rabies is a deadly neurological viral disease transmitted through the bite of an infected animal. Getting a rabies vaccination for your dog is not only safe and sensible, it is mandatory everywhere in the United States. Puppies should be immunized against this disease between 16 and 24 weeks of age.

Bordetella

Bordetella is also known as "kennel cough." This is important if your dog will be visiting a lot of other dogs or if he is going to be housed in a kennel. Many organisms can cause this condition, which is like a bad cold in older dogs but more serious in puppies. True to its name, dogs with bordetella cough, wheeze, hack, and sneeze. It can spread very rapidly through a kennel because the virus is airborne. The vaccine commonly given for kennel cough needs to be administered every six months to be effective, although it does not protect against all forms of the disease. No cure exists—only supportive treatment, and in some cases, antibiotics.

Did You Know?

Rabies is a special case since it is so deadly and can be transmitted to people. You must vaccinate your dog according to local regulations, which may stipulate that your dog be vaccinated once a year or once every three years.

Coronavirus

Coronavirus is a disease related to the human cold. Most serious in puppies, coronavirus is passed through food that has been contaminated by the feces of an infected dog. It can also be picked up from any contaminated surface that a dog may lick. It is very contagious and produces vomiting, diarrhea, and depression, symptoms similar to those of parvovirus. The stool of the dog will also be yellowish. Fortunately, this disease is not quite as severe as parvovirus, but there is no real cure—only supportive care.

Lyme Disease

Lyme disease is carried primarily by the deer tick, and it was first identified in Lyme, Connecticut in the 1970s. It is now endemic in most of the country, especially in the northeast. The incubation period is from two to five months. It causes acute, intermittent lameness and fever, as well as heart and kidney disease. If untreated, your dog can have permanent arthritis. It is advisable to give your dog this vaccine if you live in an endemic area and your dog spends a lot of time traipsing around in the woods.

PARASITES

Parasites cause problems that can result in something as simple as mild itching or something much more severe, such as death. External parasites include mites (sarcoptic, demodex, ear, or cheyletiella), fleas, and ticks. Internal parasites usually include worms like roundworm, hookworm, whipworm, and heartworm. Many of these parasites can be prevented or kept under control with preventive medications.

External Parasites

External parasites live on but not inside your dog's body. With the exception of some mites, they are usually visible.

Fleas

Fleas are truly amazing creatures. They can jump 150 times their own length, accelerate faster than a race car, and live for up to a year without eating. A female can lay 2,000 eggs in her lifetime. Despite these charming attributes, many people seem to dislike fleas. This may be because they are bloodsucking and itchy, causing allergic reactions and transmitting tapeworm along the way. They can bite people, too, although they prefer dogs. Strangely, the most common flea found on the dog is the cat flea. Besides constant scratching, a sure sign that your dog has fleas is the presence of blackish/reddish granules. These are flea feces, and they are largely composed of your dog's blood.

Nowadays, there is a plethora of information available on various anti-flea and tick programs. Flea and tick preventives come in two basic kinds: adulticides, which kill adult fleas on contact, and insect growth regulators (IGR), which prevent little fleas from growing up, thus halting the flea life cycle. IGRs don't kill adult fleas, though.

Examples of adulticides include fipronil, pyrethrins, permethrin, selamectin, and imidacloprid. The first two kill ticks as well as fleas. Selamectin is kind of a "magic bullet." It kills adult fleas and stops flea eggs from hatching. It also kills the American dog tick (but not the wood tick), ear mites, sarcoptic mange mites, and heartworm. Unlike the other chemicals, it actually enters the dog's bloodstream. IGRs include lufenuron, methoprene, and pyriproxyfen.

Vaccinating the Senior Dog

There are basically two camps of opinion regarding vaccinating older animals. Some say that older dogs have a weakened immune system and need more frequent vaccinations. Others maintain that older dogs have built up a sufficient body of immunizations through their regular vaccines, meaning they need fewer (or no) vaccinations. Discuss these options with your vet.

Check your Bulldog for parasites like fleas and ticks after returning indoors.

Some people have had luck with natural alternatives to conventional flea or tick medications. Garlic, for example, has been popular for centuries. Not all natural alternatives are equally effective, however. It's important to consult with your veterinarian before selecting a particular remedy.

Ticks

Superficially, ticks look like insects, but deep down they are arachnids, more akin to spiders than bugs. Although a tick or two doesn't seem to cause any discomfort to the affected dog the way a flea infestation does, all 850 species of tick are extremely dangerous. They carry an almost interminable list of diseases, including Lyme disease, Rocky Mountain spotted fever, ehrlichiosis, babesiosis, tularemia, and tick paralysis.

Complete tick control means controlling ticks both in the environment and on your dog. To remove ticks in the environment, remove tall bushes around the house and keep grass short. Because ticks are so dangerous, if you live in a really tick-infested area, you may have to resort to chemical control. You can use fenvalorate, which is environmentally safe (although it's not a good idea to spray it in areas where runoff could carry it to rivers or lakes). Use it every 30 days during tick season (April to November). Deer ticks are most active in the fall, so don't quit just because it gets chilly at night.

To prevent ticks on your dog, you may want to choose a monthly topical insecticide (even though ticks aren't insects). Other products contain selamectin, which controls the American dog tick. Most contain permethrin, pyrethrin, imidacloprid, or fipronil. Read all labels and follow the directions carefully. Another option is a spray that comes in an aerosol or pump bottle. Most products contain permethrin or pyrethrin. Apply on the area around the ears and eyes with a cotton ball. Tick powders containing pyrethrin are available, but they can be messy or even dangerous if inhaled. I advise against them. Dips and rinses containing permethrin, pyrethrin, or organophosphates were once very popular but have now mostly been bypassed by newer products. Finally, anti-tick collars are very effective in extremely tick-infested areas. They can be used in combination with a permethrin product for optimum results.

If a tick attacks your Bulldog, pull it off with a pair of fine-tipped tweezers. Wear gloves if possible. Don't bother trying to smother the tick with petroleum jelly or burning it. Grip it as close to the head as possible. (You want to avoid crushing the tick and forcing its bacteria-laden contents into your Bulldog.) Once the tick is out, throw it in some alcohol to kill it, or flush it down the toilet. While ticks may not die if flushed down the toilet, they're not going anywhere, either. Clean the area of the bite with a disinfectant and wash your own hands. The bite wound may develop into a welt from the tick's saliva, but this doesn't mean the tick's head is stuck in there. Give it some time; it should heal in about a week. If you believe that an infection or abscess is forming, however, take your dog to the vet.

Did You Know?

Fleas don't like heights, or at least high altitudes. If you want your dog to be flea-free without treatment, try moving to Denver.

Mites

Mites are arachnids that are related to spiders. Altogether there are over 30,000 kinds of mites, but only a dozen or so infect dogs. The following are some problems your dog may encounter if infested with mites.

• **Ear mites.** Ear mites are very small, crab-like creatures that live in the ear canals. They cause a foul odor in the ear and cause the dog to shake his head. Because these symptoms can be caused by a wide variety of problems, it is best to have the ears examined by a vet before instilling medication that can make an accurate diagnosis more difficult. Several medications are available to treat ear mites, and your veterinarian will advise what is best for your dog.

• **Demodectic mange.** Demodectic mange, also called red mange, is a fairly common skin disease that most generally affects puppies. While the culprit, Demodex canis, can be found on most dogs, only some seem to suffer adverse effects, probably due to a defective immune system. There is also a hereditary component.

When the disease is present, mites crowd out the hair follicles, causing the hair to fall out. In addition, the follicles often become infected and the skin becomes red and inflamed. A skin scraping can be made to confirm the diagnosis. Mange in puppies usually resolves itself, but it can also be treated with insecticides. If an adult dog contracts demodectic mange, it's a sign that the immune system may be compromised. Adult-onset demodectic mange is very serious and requires almost continual attention. The outcome is far from assured, however

• **Sarcoptic mange (scabies).** This is a highly contagious parasitic disease affecting both humans and dogs. The culprit is a microscopic mite called Sarcoptes scabiei. The mites burrow in the skin and cause itchiness, redness, and hair loss in both people and dogs. (This mite can affect almost any kind of animal, by the way, especially livestock.) Sarcoptic mange is treated with special shampoos, dips, pills, or injections.

Internal Parasites

Some troubling parasites, like worms and giardia, make their living inside your dog—completely invisible even to the most observant owner. The only way you will discover your dog has them is by learning how they can physically affect your pet.

Internal parasites can afflict both puppies and adult dogs, as well as people. There are dozens of varieties, and different species can infect different parts of the dog's body. A few kinds attack the esophagus and stomach, but the most common ones go for the small intestine (like roundworms, hookworms, threadworms, trichina worms, tapeworms, and flukes). Still other parasites, like whipworms, target the cecum and colon. In fact, almost every

Tick Paralysis

Tick paralysis has most frequently been reported in the western United States and Canada. The first case was reported in 1912. This condition develops after the tick has been attached to the dog for a few days. If you don't remove the tick, paralysis can develop in the neck, throat, and face of the dog, causing difficulty in chewing, swallowing, or breathing. It sounds horrible, and it is, but if you just remove the tick, the dog will make a complete recovery in 48 hours. Don't just wait to see if your dog recovers, though; have him examined by a vet, because some dogs require more aggressive therapy.

organ of the dog's body, including the liver, nasal cavity, trachea, lungs, heart, kidneys, nervous system, arteries, and veins, can be prey to one kind of worm or another.

Some worms are transmitted though food. Freezing meat to 40°F (-40°C) for two days or heating it to 140°F (60°C) kills them. Of course, finding a place to freeze anything at -40°F (-40°C) is a bit of a problem unless you live in a laboratory.

The only way to keep your dog worm-free is to use a regular dewormer on your dog (many heartworm preventives do the trick) and keep his quarters and your yard clean and picked up. When you bring your puppy to the vet for his first checkup, she should ask you to bring a stool sample, which she will inspect for internal parasites. Your vet can then periodically check your dog for evidence of parasites, and if necessary, prescribe medication to get rid of them.

Giardia (*Giardia lamblia*)

Giardia lamblia is a microscopic organism that lives in water. It can be found in the clearest mountain springs, the muddiest swamps, and even some tap water. Because it exists in water, it can also be found in food. Prevalent worldwide, giardia is the most common internal parasite of dogs. In fact, it is estimated that about 50 percent of puppies overall are affected.

Giardia attacks the intestinal tract, causing diarrhea, pain, and vomiting. Sometimes the symptoms are so subtle that owners may not even be aware that their dog is infected. People can contract giardia also, not only from drinking contaminated water but even from petting their infected dog! If the giardia lands outside the dog's body, it surrounds itself in a tough cyst that can survive for up to two months. If you pet your dog and then let the invisible cyst get near your mouth, it will live in you. A vaccine is available to protect your puppy from this infection. It can be given to puppies eight weeks of age and older.

Roundworm (*Toxocara canis*)

This is the most common worm of all. Nearly all puppies are born with roundworms, which they acquire from their mother. Roundworms penetrate the small intestine and can be carried through the bloodstream to the liver, lungs, and even up the trachea, where they are swallowed. At this point in time, the worms

Pyrethrins

Pyrethrins have been used to kill insects for over 100 years. They are made from the extracts of chrysanthemums and have a wide safety margin. A synthetic compound similar to pyrethrins is permethrin. It lasts a lot longer than pyrethrins but cannot be used on cats.

begin their life cycle all over again, producing eggs that are excreted with the feces. The worms can move to muscle tissue, where they form cysts and go dormant. Older dogs are less likely to be infected, but they can pick them up from contaminated soil.

Hookworm (Ancylostoma caninum)

Hookworms attach to the intestinal wall with their teeth and cause intestinal bleeding. The larvae are deposited in feces, where they can be easily picked up

To avoid worms, keep your yard clean.

again, either through the skin or by mouth. They like shady, sandy areas best, so barefoot children are especially at risk. Remember, hookworms don't have to be swallowed; the larvae can actually penetrate the skin and cause lesions. Dogs infected by hookworms can develop chronic intestinal bleeding and consequent pain and anemia. Because the worms absorb nutrients, they can also cause malnutrition.

Whipworm (Trichuris vulpis)

Whipworms are one of the most difficult of all worms to destroy. Their eggs seem impervious to time and cold weather, and a female whipworm can lay 2,000 eggs a day. Those aren't good statistics. Severe infestations can give a dog a terrible case of colitis, and they can even be fatal.

Tapeworm (Dipylidium caninum)

Tapeworm eggs may be found in feces or around your dog's anal opening. Tapeworm is spread by fleas. Although not as serious in dogs as in people, tapeworm requires a special dewormer to get rid of it. Dogs may not have overt signs of tapeworms other than the telltale eggs in the feces, but they should be eliminated as soon

Heartworms were first identified in the United States in 1856, but nobody seemed to notice until 1973, when the American Veterinary Medical Association first published guidelines on its treatment and prevention.

as possible because they compete for nutrients. They can also migrate into the bile duct, causing liver problems. Often, however, tapeworms seem to live rather amicably inside the dog.

Another common species, *Taenia pisiformis,* can be picked up by ingesting infected rabbits and rodents.

Ringworm (Microsporum canis)

Despite its name, ringworm is a fungus, and a highly contagious one at that. Dogs can pick it up from an infected dog or even from the ground. It is more common in puppies than in adult dogs. Classical signs include scabs or an irregularly shaped area of skin infection (not always a ring). There may be rapid hair loss at the site. People, especially children, can get ringworm from dogs, so get it treated immediately.

The specific treatment for your dog will depend on the severity of the infection, how many pets are involved, if there are children in the household, and how difficult it will be to disinfect your dog's environment. The most common treatment is griseofulvin, an oral medication.

Heartworm (Dirofilaria immitis)

Besides the normal round of vaccinations, it's critically important to keep your dog on year-round heartworm preventive, especially if you live in the southern portion of the United States. Heartworms are big creatures related to roundworms that live in the right side and large blood vessels of the heart, causing them to become obstructed. Badly infected dogs can have hundreds of these worms residing in their hearts, and they can live there for years. They lay very tiny larvae called microfilariae that can live up to three years in the bloodstream. When they reproduce, their offspring, in the form of microfilariae, circulate in the bloodstream where they can be sucked up by mosquitoes, where they then develop further. Later, they migrate to the mosquito's mouth and enter a new host.

It takes six to seven months between the time when an animal was bitten until the adult heartworms develop. Signs of infection include coughing, fluid accumulation, decreased appetite, and heart failure. Various tests are used to detect infection. When left untreated, this disease is nearly always fatal.

Treatment for heartworm is risky, long, and difficult, but it is better than dying from the disease. The treatment itself is a two-step process, as the adult worms and the microfilaria must be killed separately. (No one medication kills both.) The adults are treated first, and then a different treatment is used to kill the microfilaria and migrating larvae. As the worms die, they lodge in the lung arteries and block even more blood vessels than before treatment. The inflammation is then amplified because of the decomposing worms inside the blood vessels. Powerful medication will rid your dog of the heartworm, but it is a treatment with risks. (This is why the best "cure" for heartworm is prevention of the disease in the first place.) Your vet can prescribe a preventive medication that will keep your precious Bulldog free of heartworm. Any dog can get heartworm from even one mosquito bite, so take the safe path and keep your dog on medication. The medication will kill immature heartworms but can't be used to kill adult worms. It works by immediately killing any heartworm larvae acquired within the previous 30 days. It's best to keep your dog on year-round preventive. Heartworm medication also prevents your dog from acquiring hookworms, roundworms, and whipworms.

Heartworm Prevention

Treatment for heartworm is difficult. It's best to prevent the worms in the first place by using a year-round heartworm preventative.

COMMON DISEASES

In this section, we'll look at several common diseases of dogs, arranged according to the system that the disease affects.

Cancer

Cancer isn't really one disease. It's a general term for more than 200 different types of malignancies that can affect any part of the body. All cancers, however, work basically the same way: They result from too rapid cell growth—the cells are all "undifferentiated," meaning that they can no longer be recognized as a liver cell, skin cell, or whatever kind of cell they were supposed to be. Cancer cells also have apparently developed something like an "immortality gene," and so unlike normal cells that are born and die, cancer cells just go on indefinitely.

New treatments for cancer are on the horizon. One promising new route that is still in its experimental stage is brachytherapy. In this procedure, doctors introduce radiation-emitting beads directly into the tumor site using a hollow tube. This operation lets the doctor target the cancer directly without affecting other tissues. It is important to realize that no one cancer treatment is right for every dog. Age and even personality type may dictate the best kind of treatment. Costs can also vary widely, ranging from little more than average surgery or medication costs to several thousand dollars.

Eye Disorders

People used to believe that dogs could see in black and white only. We now know that dogs can see color, although not exactly the way people do. Dogs can see various shades of blue and can even distinguish among different shades of gray that people see as one color. However, dogs cannot distinguish between red, yellow, orange, and green, which is pretty simple for most of us.

Unfortunately, dogs can contract various different types of eye disorders, including many of the same ones that affect people, like cataracts and glaucoma. The most common ones are listed here.

Irritation

To relieve eye irritation due to smoke, dust, wind, or pollen, rinse the eyes with a clear solution made for ophthalmic use. You can even use contact lens drops.

Cherry Eye (Eversion of the Nictitating Membrane)

This common problem in Bulldogs is due to the extrusion of a gland that normally stays under the lower eyelid at the inside corner of the eye. It appears as a round, red mass. It looks terrible and should be surgically restored to its normal position. (The gland should not be removed, however, as doing so will result in "dry eye," a painful and serious condition.)

SARD

SARD is the acronym for Sudden Acquired Retinal Degeneration. It is indeed sudden, often literally striking overnight and blinding your dog, although in some cases it takes a week or even two to develop. Other senses may also be dulled. The condition is painless and may be

Common Signs

According to the Veterinary Cancer Society, here are common signs of cancer in small animals (and notice how similar these signs are to cancer in human beings):

- Abnormal swellings that persist or continue to grow
- Sores that don't heal
- Weight loss
- Loss of appetite
- Bleeding or discharge from any body opening
- Offensive odor
- Difficulty eating or swallowing
- Hesitation to exercise or loss of stamina
- Persistent lameness or stiffness
- Difficulty breathing, urinating, or defecating

If your Bulldog displays unusual behavior for more than a few days, such as lethargy or listlessness, a trip to the vet might be in order.

accompanied by weight gain, increased appetite, and thirst. Any breed can be affected, and most victims are females between the ages of 7 and 14. The cause is unknown, but stress, lawn pesticides, and autoimmune disease may all be implicated. There is no cure or treatment for this disease at the present time.

Entropion

In this condition, which is common in Bulldogs, the lower (usually) eyelid rolls inward and brings the lashes into direct contact with the cornea. It is very irritating to the eye. Many dogs are born with entropion, but it can also be acquired later in life as a result of corneal eye disease or other causes. One or both eyes may be affected. Signs of entropion include tearing, squinting, rubbing, discharge, and rolling of the eyelid. Surgical treatment is the only cure, but it needs to be done by a veterinarian experienced in the procedure. (Overcorrection leads to other problems.) After surgery, your Bulldog will probably wear a special collar to prevent him from reinjuring the eye. Sometimes antibiotics will be prescribed as well. Because this is an inherited condition, affected animals should not be bred.

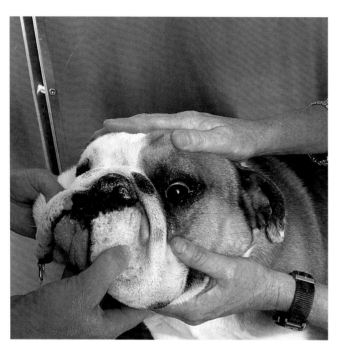

Your vet can check for common eye ailments at your Bulldog's annual physical exam.

Glaucoma

Glaucoma is a painful condition that occurs when pressure inside the eyeball increases to dangerous levels. This is the most common cause of blindness in dogs and cats. It occurs when the small drainage sties within the eyeball are narrowed or blocked. The result is usually permanent damage to the retina, causing severe pain and blindness. Often the cause is heritable, but the disease can also result from injury, tumors, or infections.

Glaucoma is a veterinary emergency that requires immediate attention to have any chance of saving the eye. Signs include squinting, drainage, and sometimes swelling of the eye. Diagnosis is based on pressure measurement of the eyes, although other tests may be used to find underlying causes. Blood work, an ultrasound, and CAT scans may also be used to determine underlying causes. If blindness results, the eye may be injected with an agent that removes the pressure; however, the dog will remain blind. Sometimes a severely damaged eye must be surgically removed. The goal of both procedures is to relieve pain.

Blindness

Any number of conditions can produce blindness, including glaucoma, retinal disease, trauma, cataracts, and corneal problems. While it's certainly no fun, blindness is not the tragedy for dogs that it is for many humans. Most dogs make a remarkable adjustment, and their owners are usually more traumatized than the dogs. Some owners make the mistake of carrying their dogs around. Don't do this; let your Bulldog learn to navigate on his own—it'll be an adventure for him. Use a lead to take him to new places.

While dogs do depend on their eyes, they have keen ears and a good nose to considerably make up for their loss of sight. Dogs who lose their vision suddenly have more problems than others, but even these dogs eventually come around and return to a normal doggy life. Some dogs who go blind slowly adapt so well that their owners are unaware of the fact that darkness has finally fallen. These owners may not figure it out until they change the furniture around.

To help your dog adjust, maintain as much stability in the home as possible. Keep furniture shifting to a minimum, and if you do have to move it, take the dog around so he learns the new arrangement. Even leaving a relatively small thing in an unaccustomed place may cause some confusion. Protect your dog by removing dangerous objects and covering spas or other tubs of water that he might tumble into. Put a "blind dog" tag on his collar so that if he becomes lost, the finder will have a clue as to his condition.

Some dogs learn to navigate by holding a buffering object like a stuffed toy as they move from place to place. You can even purchase a special device that fits around the dog and protects him. Most dogs learn to navigate their own environments so well that they don't need this, however.

Because a blind dog can't see you, it's wise to speak before touching him (and shocking the heck out of him). Feed him at the same time in the same place every day and supervise his outdoor activity.

Ear Infections

Signs of an ear infection include pawing at the ears, as well as tilting or shaking the head. The ears themselves will probably give off a foul odor. For most cases of ear infection, your vet will prescribe a medication that can be applied to the ear. (Some infections are bacterial, some are fungal, and some are a mixture of both, so using the correct medication is important.)

For dogs with chronic infections, the vet may want to flush the ear out under anesthesia. It is too painful to be done well when the animal is awake. Afterward, you'll need to clean and treat the ear daily. If the infection subsides, the ear must still be cleaned for the rest of the dog's life.

Allergies

Like people, dogs suffer from various allergies. In most cases,

Allergies

The most common allergies affecting dogs are:

- Atopic dermatitis
- Contact allergy
- Flea allergy
- Food allergy
- Hot spots
- Insect stings

allergic reactions are annoying but not life-threatening. Your dog doesn't usually sneeze when he has an allergy, however. Sometimes allergies express themselves as urticaria (hives) or angioedema. Urticaria is a condition characterized by small bumps in the skin and is a typical hypersensitive or allergic reaction. Sometimes the bumps are itchy, but not always. A related condition is angioedema, or swelling of the face, especially around the muzzle and eyes. These reactions typically develop within 20 minutes of exposure to the allergen. They aren't usually life-threatening, although severe swelling around the throat can make breathing even more difficult for a Bulldog. The treatment is generally antihistamines, but if breathing is affected, epinephrine is administered.

One of the most severe allergic reactions is anaphylaxis, a life-threatening condition that may include shock, respiratory and cardiac failure, and death. Anything that can cause an allergic reaction can cause anaphylaxis, including insect stings, antibiotics, vaccines or other medications, and even foods. It is rare but deadly. Common signs include sudden diarrhea, vomiting, pale gums, fast heart rate, shock, seizures, coma, and death. Unlike many other kinds of allergic reactions, there is no facial swelling. This is an extreme emergency—your dog needs epinephrine right away. Immediately drive to the nearest vet clinic. Intravenous fluids, oxygen, and other medications may also be needed. While it is not known exactly what may cause animals to react so badly, dogs who have previously had an allergic reaction (like hives) are most at risk. If your dog suffers severe allergic reactions that affect his breathing, you may be able to secure an "epi-pen" from your vet, a syringe and needle containing a single dose of epinephrine for future emergencies.

There's no real cure for allergies, but several treatment options are available, ranging from avoiding the allergen (not easy), to administering special shampoos and oils, to dispensing medications. Check with your vet to determine the best option for you and your Bulldog.

The following are some of the most common allergies affecting dogs.

Atopic Dermatitis

Atopic dermatitis (AD) is a very common skin condition in dogs caused by airborne allergens like dust mites, mold, or pollen. While some dogs seem to be able to tolerate a lot of that stuff, others can't—just like people. The first clinical signs of AD appear when the dog is between six months and three years of age.

In the beginning, you will likely notice that your dog seems to be itchy; he may rub his face or lick his feet. Then, you may observe some red-looking spots around the place where the dog encountered the allergen. Reddened, irritated skin and skin lesions occur due to scratching at and chewing on those itchy areas. AD is often worse during the summer, when pollen and mold levels increase.

Dogs can develop allergies to mold and pollen.

The preferred method of handling this and any allergy is to remove the allergen from the dog. With fleas, this is comparatively easy—with pollen, it isn't. In some cases, your dog can receive a series of shots to help build up resistance, but it's not a guarantee.

Contact Allergy

In this kind of allergy, the dog reacts to an irritant that actually touches the skin. It is not as common as AD.

Flea Allergy

This is one of the most common canine allergies. Some dogs start itching madly after one flea bite. The obvious way to handle it is to make sure your dog doesn't get fleas.

Food Allergy

A food allergy is a reaction to an ingredient in your dog's food. Dogs with food allergies may scratch at their faces. Treatment involves finding the source of the allergy and removing it from the

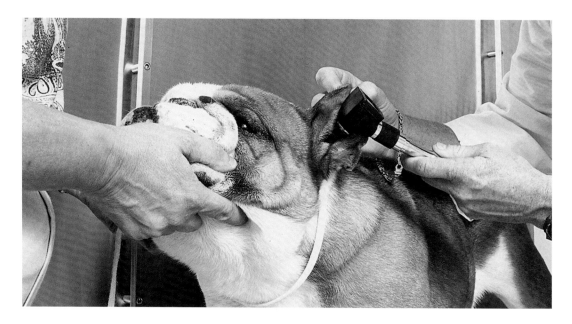

diet. In most cases, the villain is a protein, usually beef or chicken. In other cases, wheat or soy is to blame.

Hot Spots

These frightening-looking skin sores are usually caused by irritation, allergies, or dirt in the skin. The dog will scratch himself and make the condition worse by infecting the sores. If hot spots appear, wash them thoroughly with shampoo, rinse, and dry them. You may want to use a drying powder you can obtain from your vet.

Insect Stings

Unless your dog has a serious allergic reaction, a bee sting can be treated with an over-the-counter antihistamine, broken open and applied to the sting site. If your dog's breathing becomes labored, however, he may be having an allergic reaction—get him to the vet right away.

Skin Disorders

Acne

Some Bulldogs seem prone to pimples, which form on the chin or abdomen. You can usually clear them up with an over-the-counter anti-acne cream for people, such as a benzoyl peroxide cream applied twice daily. In other cases, your vet will prescribe an oral or cream topical antibiotic. This isn't a life-threatening disease, but it can be irritating to your dog. "Puppy acne" is common in many breeds, but in Bulldogs, the condition may continue into adulthood.

Interdigital Cysts

These are chronic swellings that occur between the toes. The cysts are filled with an inflammatory fluid that is forced deep into the tissues. The cause is unknown. In a very few cases, you can treat them by soaking the paw in warm water and Epsom salts, then drying it and applying a medication recommended by your vet. Most of the time, however, interdigital cysts must be removed surgically.

Itching (Pruritus)

Itching is really a symptom, not a disease in itself. However, when a dog starts scratching from whatever cause, he can inflame the skin even further. Some dogs have a higher "itch threshold" than others and almost never scratch, no matter what torments them. For others, it's the least little thing. (It's the same with people.) Itching can be especially serious with Bulldogs, because some of them have a tendency toward self-mutilation.

Bacterial or yeast infections, hot spots, skin parasites (mites and fleas), pyoderma, and allergies are major causes of itching. If your dog starts itching, check some of these probable causes. If your dog is clean and parasite-free, consult your vet and investigate the matter further.

Lick Granuloma

If your dog suffers from lick granuloma, you may notice that he is licking himself raw. While it may have begun in response to a sore foot (although this is not always the case), it may have turned into a nervous habit, like nail biting in people. There also seems to be a genetic component. Most foot gnawers have experienced a stressful situation at home, such as the addition or loss of a family member, a period of lengthy confinement, or boredom. However, it's recently been suggested that a nervous or obsessive-compulsive disorder may also be responsible. (These things are always tricky.

Deafness

Deafness is a common problem in Bulldogs. There is a link between a predominantly white coat (especially around the head) and loss of hearing. (The same condition is seen in Dalmatians, Boxers, and Bull Terriers.) No one really knows the reason, but it appears that during the embryo stage, pigment cells migrate or interact somehow with structures in the inner ear. During the first few weeks of life, the structures of the cochlea (the principal organ of hearing in the ear) degenerate. The condition may occur in one or both ears. The condition manifests itself by four weeks of age, and testing may be safely done after five weeks of age. The test used to confirm deafness is the BAER test, which can be performed without sedation.

A deaf dog can make a perfectly satisfactory pet, and many can learn hand signals with remarkable ease.

Many conditions begin as physical problems and then become psychological or vice versa.)

This is a frustrating disease to treat, and every dog needs to be assessed individually. The first step is usually to treat the dog's foot; the second is to treat the dog's mental state. For the foot, the veterinarian may prescribe a long-acting corticosteroid to stop the itching. A biopsy is recommended to confirm the diagnosis, as other conditions may appear similar. She may add wraps for the foot, an Elizabethan collar to protect it, and topical corticosteroid creams. Some dogs may also need antibiotics or other drugs.

To help your dog's mental state, you may need to do nothing more than pay more attention to him and give him things to do. This is usually a successful approach in the early stages of the problem. However, if it has developed into an obsessive-compulsive disorder, you may have to result to psychoactive drugs. Some people even swear by acupuncture. Contact your vet for more information on these treatment options.

Skinfold Dermatitis

Skinfold dermatitis is an inflammation of the facial wrinkles or wrinkles elsewhere on the body. It is common in Bulldogs, especially around the face and in the tail pocket. In some cases, the nasal folds that form just in front of the eye can be so pronounced that they actually rub against the cornea. Dogs with this condition will have watery, red, or infected eyes. The only treatment is surgery to remove, or at least decrease, the size of the folds.

Cardiovascular Diseases

Aortic Stenosis

Bulldogs are prone to aortic stenosis, a narrowing of the pathway for blood leaving the heart. Usually this narrowing occurs beneath the aortic valve of the left ventricle, in which case it is referred to as subvalvular aortic stenosis (SAS). Bulldogs are one of the breeds most disposed to this genetic condition. In a mild case, there may merely be a heart murmur. More serious cases can lead to exercise intolerance, fainting, heart failure, and even sudden death. Undue difficulty in breathing, coughing, or fainting should prompt a visit to your veterinarian. In dogs with moderate or severe stenosis, exercise should be restricted. Sometimes beta-blocking drugs are helpful, but there is no way to cure the disease.

Congestive Heart Failure

Heart failure is caused by some abnormality in heart function or structure. Dogs with heart failure have less blood pumped to the muscles. It often leads to fluid retention in the lung or body cavity, a condition called "congestive heart failure," and causes difficulty breathing. Some kinds of heart failure are due to birth defects. In other cases, the heart valves degenerate. Heartworms can cause it, as can diseases of the lining around the heart. Dogs of any age or breed can develop the disease. Signs of heart failure include coughing, shortness of breath, difficult breathing, weight loss, and fatigue.

Some dogs with congestive heart failure fail to eat well, or show signs of muscle wasting. A low-sodium diet is best, but many dogs just won't eat that kind of food (which will consist mostly of vegetables). All commercial foods contain too much sodium for dogs with heart failure. However, it probably helps to add fish oil, which is loaded with important omega-3 fatty acids, to the diet. Of course, if your pet is overweight, put him on a diet to reduce the stress on his heart.

Bulldogs are prone to respiratory problems like dyspnea, elongated palate, and stenotic nares.

Respiratory Disorders

Dyspnea

Dyspnea is a fancy term for difficult breathing. It is not a disease in and of itself but is a sign of another problem. Dyspnea may result from heart or lung disease, pressure on the airway, infections, fluid retention, or trauma. Bulldogs are very prone to this problem. Treatment, if any, depends on the cause of the disease, so consult your vet to find out your options.

Bordetella (Kennel Cough)

Bordetella is a dog's version of the common cold. It is an airborne virus that in itself is not usually serious (although it is serious in puppies). It occurs mostly in kenneled dogs, is highly contagious, and can occur in combination with distemper, adenovirus, and parainfluenza. Symptoms include a harsh cough, often with gagging and nasal discharge of varying colors. In animals with a healthy immune system, kennel cough lasts for five to seven days. In young or weak dogs, it may last much longer. In some cases, kennel cough can lead to pneumonia, which requires intensive, prolonged treatment.

There are vaccines available for bordetella; some are intranasal, while others are injectable. They have to be given rather frequently, but even vaccination against one strain of the disease is no guarantee that your dog won't become infected with a different variety.

Kennel cough can be treated with a combination of a cough suppressant and antibiotics, but there is no cure. It just has to run its course, like a cold. However, just because your dog is coughing doesn't mean he has kennel cough. It could be something more serious, so be sure to consult with your veterinarian.

Elongated Palate

This is a very common problem in Bulldogs. The soft palate is the flap of skin at the back of your dog's throat. If it is too long, it will block the airway, making it hard for your Bulldog to breathe. Bulldogs are subject to this congenital deformity. Your dog may gasp and wheeze even more than is "normal" for a Bulldog. An elongated palate can make even eating and drinking difficult, causing your dog to choke easily or spit up bits of food. In some cases, the dog can even faint.

If your dog has this problem, check with your vet. She will look down the throat (usually while the dog is awake) to determine the nature and extent of the problem. It can be corrected with surgery, although you'll have to wait until the dog is about a year old and finished

Because itching can be especially serious in Bulldogs, you should immediately check for parasites or a bacterial infection if he appears to be constantly scratching.

growing. Most vets now use laser surgery for this procedure, which cauterizes while it cuts, thus minimizing swelling and bleeding and shortening recovery time. While your dog heals, feed him only soft food.

Stenotic Nares (Constricted Nostrils)

This birth defect occurs only among brachycephalic, short-snouted dogs like the Bulldog. It occurs when the cartilage that helps to shape the nostrils is too soft. As the puppy breathes, the nostril collapses and severely restricts airflow. Signs can include labored breathing, snoring, breathing from the mouth, and a watery or foamy discharge from the nostrils. In severe cases, the puppy's chest even becomes flattened. Puppies with this condition are treated surgically as soon as possible by removing a section of the nasal cartilage to enlarge the nostril openings.

Bone and Joint Disorders

Most Bulldogs, and indeed most dogs, will develop some kind of joint disease during their lives that will usually appear as they grow older. Signs of joint disease include stiffness, limping, or favoring a limb. You may notice your dog's reluctance to climb stairs, jump, or even get up. Causes of such pain can include arthritis, dysplasia, Lyme disease, intervertebral disk disease, tendon or muscle disease, fractures, and obesity.

Arthritis

Signs of arthritis include stiffness, exercise intolerance, reluctance to climb stairs, and difficulty getting up or down. They are similar to the symptoms that people display.

One important step in controlling arthritis in pets is good weight management. It is harder to keep a Bulldog on a diet than it is to give him a pill, but it's really worth it. Moderate daily, controlled exercise is important as well. Look for activities that provide good range of motion without putting stress on the joints. Regular

walking around the block at a sensible pace has many benefits; don't try to "catch up" on weekends by overdoing it. Stick to a realistic daily schedule.

Make sure your arthritic Bulldog has a warm, draft-free sleeping area, and if it is really cold, buy or knit him a sweater to keep those old joints warm and snug. Spend a little extra to buy him an orthopedic bed that distributes weight properly. Also, try to learn enough massage and physical therapy to help his muscles and joints relax. Gentle kneading of affected joints using a circular motion will make your dog feel better. You may even want to apply moist heat.

You can also help your pet by making his routine activities easier. Ramps can help older dogs go up and down short flights of stairs or into cars. You can also make drinking bowls more accessible by placing them in every room. Some dogs are so stiff that they don't get enough water simply because it's too hard for them to get to it.

While many arthritic dogs are routinely put on carprofen or a similar drug, a study in the United Kingdom has shown that high-quality glucosamine with chondroitin sulfate provides the same pain relief. Glucosamine helps in the synthesis and maintenance of cartilage in the joint, while chondroitin enhances the synthesis of

A common genetic cause of rear leg lameness, hip dysplasia affects a large number of Bulldogs.

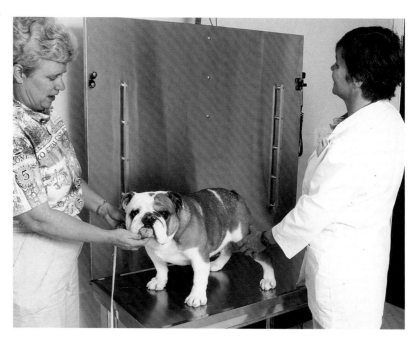

glycosaminoglycans and inhibits damaging enzymes in the joint. These substances aren't painkillers; they actually heal the damage. They are very safe, with no side effects. The big drawback to glucosamine is the inconsistency of the products—not everything you get off the shelf really works. Purity and usability vary widely. Check with your vet to obtain pharmaceutical-quality products.

Another natural source for arthritis relief is the green-lipped mussel (Perna canaliculus), an edible shellfish found off the shores of New Zealand. The soft tissue is processed into a powder containing glycosaminoglycans (GAGs, the main components of cartilage and the joint fluid), eicosatetraenoic acids (ETAs), and glucosamine, which helps reduce inflammation.

Your veterinarian may have other suggestions, including anti-inflammatory drugs that can be used with glucosamine/chondroitin products. Corticosteroids and aspirin are seldom prescribed nowadays because of their side effects and because other drugs work better.

No Jumping!

Don't allow your young Bulldog to jump on and off furniture, because it is very bad for his growing bones. He could develop carpal injuries or a severe sprain. The Bulldog's body cannot withstand jumping well.

Hip Dysplasia

Hip dysplasia is a common, genetic cause of rear leg lameness. It's actually a juvenile bone disease because it usually first shows up between 6 and 18 months, although early signs can be very subtle.

While this disease is mostly associated with large-breed dogs, the Orthopedic Foundation for Animals (OFA) found that 75 percent of Bulldogs were considered dysplastic, and zero percent were rated "excellent." In fact, the OFA rates Bulldogs as being the breed most likely to have hip dysplasia. Some Bulldog breeders dispute this claim, saying that the loose joint is normal for the breed. Very few Bulldog breeders actually submit their dogs for hip evaluations, partly because almost all Bulldogs are dysplastic by OFA standards and partly because the test requires anesthesia, which is dangerous for Bulldogs. In any event, severe cases of hip dysplasia require surgery, usually a total hip replacement or a triple pelvic osteotomy.

Lyme Disease

Lyme disease is spread by ticks and can affect many body systems. Its main manifestation, however, is an acute or recurrent arthritis. The actual culprit is the microscopic spirochete *Borrelia burgdorferi*. Puppies may be at increased risk. Signs of Lyme disease include lameness, pain, joint swelling, fever, and depression. Lyme disease is treated with a course of antibiotics.

Disk Disease

Intervertebral disks are almost like shock absorbers between the vertebrae in the spine. The outside of each disk (the annulus fibrosis) is tough and fibrous, but inside the disk (the nucleus pulposus), it's more like a gel. As your dog ages, the disks becomes less resilient, and they are more likely to rupture. This is what's sometimes called a slipped disk, even though nothing has actually slipped. Surgery is frequently required in more serious cases. In less severe cases, the dog may recover by himself.

Renal System Disorders

The renal system consists of the kidneys and urinary bladder. Its purpose is to cleanse the blood of toxins and other undesirable substances and excrete them from the body.

Bladder Stones

One of the most common problems of the renal system is bladder stones (uroliths), which come about when the dog's urine is saturated with excess minerals like magnesium, phosphorus, calcium, or ammonia. Bladder stones can often be prevented and are sometimes eliminated through a diet change, although some kinds are formed in the presence of bacteria such as E. coli, Staph. spp., and proteus. Some diseases, such as liver shunts, or even some medications, are also associated with the manifestation of bladder stones.

One way to check if your dog is in danger of bladder stones is to measure his urine pH, which indicates acidity. A pH of 7 is neutral. Some bladder stones tend to form in more alkaline urine, and others form in more acid urine.

To help prevent your dog from getting bladder stones, make

sure he is allowed to urinate when he needs to. Keeping dogs locked up in the house for many hours a day without the chance to urinate is not only very uncomfortable for your dog, but it is just asking for bladder stones. Your dog also needs access to fresh water at all times.

Dogs with bladder stones may require surgery.

Chronic Renal Disease

Chronic renal disease is a common problem in older Bulldogs. It has no specific cause but occurs when the filtration areas or glomeruli inside the kidney deteriorate and can no longer remove normal wastes from the bloodstream. Symptoms of chronic renal disease develop slowly over time and may include excessive thirst, an increase in the amount of urine voided, and house soiling. Later problems may include vomiting, loss of appetite, and mouth ulcers. There's no cure, but obtaining special diets from your veterinarian can slow down the process.

Nervous System Disorders

Canine Cognitive Dysfunction (CCD)

Canine cognitive dysfunction, also referred to as cognitive dysfunction syndrome, is the most common ailment that affects the nervous system. It is signaled by a decline in learning, memory, and perception. Dogs with this disease tend to wander aimlessly, bark for no reason, forget housetraining, and become distant from their families. It has been successfully treated with l-deprenyl, an enzyme inhibitor; the drug is also used to treat Parkinson's disease. The addition of vitamins C and E, l-carnitine, lipoic acid, and fish oils may also help. There is even a diet available that has been

Rabies

Rabies is a 100 percent fatal disease affecting the nerves and brain, and it is the law in the United States that dogs be vaccinated for it. It is caused by a virus usually carried by raccoons, foxes, skunks, and bats, and it is usually transmitted through a bite.

The most common sign of rabies in dogs is a behavior change: A friendly dog will turn wild, or a wild animal will appear tame. By the time this change shows up, however, the animal may have already been infected for months. Once the signs appear, the animal will be dead within a matter of days.

specifically designed to help dogs with cognitive dysfunction syndrome.

Epilepsy

This brain disorder can affect any breed, although most researchers strongly suspect a genetic link. No one, however, really knows what causes epilepsy, which is why it is known as "idiopathic epilepsy," a seizure without a known cause. For a dog to be accurately diagnosed with epilepsy, other diseases must be ruled out first. These other diseases include thyroid dysfunction, head trauma, kidney or liver disease, calcium deficiency, toxins, diabetes, hypoglycemia, brain tumors, and allergies. Encourage your vet to test for these other possibilities, especially thyroid problems, which are easily diagnosed with a special blood screening.

Epilepsy often first appears in dogs between one and three years of age. The main symptom is a seizure, either a partial seizure or a full seizure. Most seizures are quite brief, ranging between 45 seconds and 3 minutes. With partial seizures, the dog may not even lose consciousness but will simply shake his head or even run around frantically. Occasionally, however, long seizures lasting 20 minutes or more can occur in waves. This is a life-threatening situation, as the blood supply to the brain and other vital organs can be disrupted.

Although there is no cure for epilepsy, many treatments, including medication and lifestyle changes, can help. The most common drug therapy is phenobarbital, which is inexpensive. However, it can be hard on the liver, so some veterinarians are having luck with potassium bromide, which is safer, as well

Seizures

If your dog is having a seizure, don't panic! It will probably last only a few minutes, although your dog may not seem "right" for some time following. If the seizure goes on for ten minutes, however, transport your dog to your vet, as irreversible brain damage can occur.

Remember the following points if your Bulldog suffers from a seizure:

- Don't place anything in your dog's mouth during a seizure. He won't swallow his tongue, but you can get badly bitten if you start fooling around with his mouth.

- Note down the time of the seizure, how long it lasts, and all relevant circumstances.

- Take all information regarding the seizure with you to the vet. It may help her determine the cause.

as some other medications. Even more promising is diazepam (Valium), which is used for cluster seizures. One of the great things about this medication is that it can be administered at home. Recurrent seizures usually require lifetime medication, which can be administered at home.

Unfortunately, about 30 percent of epileptic dogs do not respond well to drug therapy, and in these cases, owners just learn how to handle seizures as they occur. In most cases, the seizures are more frightening to the owner than to the dog. However, holistic veterinarians are trying other methods of treatment that may prove beneficial. These include homeopathic remedies, diet therapy, ear acupuncture, gold bead implants, herbal treatments, and vitamin supplementation. Vitamins A, C, E, and choline have proved particularly helpful.

Endocrine System Disorders

Diabetes

About 1 in every 200 dogs will develop diabetes. Signs include excessive thirst, excessive urination, excessive appetite, and weight loss despite good appetite. It's most common in female dogs between seven and nine years of age. The treatment is the same as for humans—insulin. Currently, the Food and Drug Administration (FDA) has announced a porcine (pig) insulin zinc suspension product, Vetsulin, as the first drug specifically approved for treating dogs. Prior to this, veterinarians had to use human insulin, which is less compatible with a dog's metabolic system. This product will be available by prescription.

The kidneys are marvelously efficient. Over 75 percent of their function can be decreased before they are no longer able to detoxify the body!

Pancreatitis

The pancreas is a little organ tucked up under the stomach and small intestine. It produces enzymes needed to digest food and hormones, including insulin. Because we need all of this to live, the pancreas is pretty important!

Pancreatitis occurs when the pancreas becomes inflamed (in fact, "itis" means "inflammation") and starts leaking digestive enzymes, which can start digesting the pancreas itself. Some types of pancreatitis happen overnight, while others take a long time to develop. Both can be life-threatening.

Unfortunately, we don't usually know what causes pancreatitis,

Megaesophagus

In this condition, which can be congenital or acquired, the esophagus is enlarged. This is a very serious condition that leads to regurgitation of food, and consequently, aspiration pneumonia. There is no cure, but it can sometimes be managed by raising the dog's feeding position.

although certain risk factors have been identified. These include high fat content in the blood, obesity, infection, contaminated food, certain other diseases like diabetes or Cushing's disease, and the use of some prescription drugs. A high-fat meal just before the onset of the disease is also common. A dog with pancreatitis may vomit, avoid food, have a change in body temperature (up or down), and experience pain in the abdomen. He may also stand in a "hunched" position. Diarrhea and depression are common as well, as is dehydration. None of these signs, however, is a sure sign of pancreatitis; the disease is notoriously hard to diagnose. Your vet will run tests that include a check on the pancreatic enzymes for more clues. She may also take x-rays.

The only treatment for pancreatitis is supportive therapy, which usually includes feeding through IVs for a few days in order to rest the digestive system. Afterward, your Bulldog will probably be placed on a low-fat diet.

Cushing's Disease (Hyperadrenocorticism)

With this condition, the adrenal gland overproduces corticosteroids. Signs include increased appetite and thirst, excessive urination, muscle wasting, and panting. The dog may have fluid accumulating in the abdomen. Cushing's can be treated either medically (through the use of several drug therapies) or with surgery.

Digestive System Disorders

The digestive system handles processing food from its point of consumption to its excretion from the body. Unfortunately, things can go wrong anywhere along the way.

Dental Disease

The good news is that your Bully is unlikely to get cavities. The bad news is that he is liable to experience gum disease and tartar buildup. Bad things start to happen when plaque (a sticky mixture of food particles and bacteria) starts to accumulate on the surface of the teeth. You can get rid of it with daily brushing, but if you don't, minerals in the saliva combine with plaque and form tartar or calculus, a combination of calcium phosphate and carbonate and plaque. It sticks to the tooth surface and forms a scaffold for the accumulation of even more tartar.

It only takes two or three days of not brushing for tartar to begin destroying your dog's teeth. You can't get rid of tartar by brushing, because at this point it's too late. Tartar doesn't feel good either. It's quite irritating to the gums and causes a nasty inflammation called gingivitis.

In later stages, tartar builds up under the gum and separates the gum from the teeth, which will eventually loosen and fall out. Even jaw fracture can result. This is periodontal disease, and unfortunately, it's irreversible, painful, and dangerous. Periodontal disease inflames and destroys the structures that support the teeth. It is also the number one source of the bacteria that cause aspiration pneumonia. The bacteria can invade the blood stream and wreak havoc on the heart valves, liver, and kidneys.

Signs of periodontal disease usually include the following, although some signs are not apparent except with an x-ray or professional exam:

Does your Bulldog have bad breath? He may be suffering from dental disease.

- Bleeding gums
- Gum inflammation (gingivitis)
- Chattering
- Drooling
- Lack of appetite and less interest in chewing
- Loose teeth
- Pawing at face
- Bad breath (halitosis)
- Choosing softer foods

You don't want your dog to have to experience periodontal disease. It's completely preventable. How? Brush your Bulldog's teeth every day and give him toys and treats that aid in the prevention of periodontal disease, like strong Nylabones. Also, take him to the vet for a complete dental workup twice a year. This is more often than some other breeds may need, but Bulldogs are

prone to tooth-crowding and are thus more likely to be victims of periodontal disease.

Gastric Dilatation Volvulus (Bloat or G.D.V.)

In this condition, the stomach fills up with fluid and gas. If the stomach twists, which is common, a life-threatening emergency will ensue that requires immediate veterinary care. Signs of bloat can include attempts to vomit, hypersalivation, restlessness, and abdominal distention. Dogs who eat very fast and who belch or are flatulent are at increased risk.

A study published in the Journal of the American Animal Hospital Association reports that dogs fed a larger volume of food per meal (based on the median number of cups fed per kilogram of body weight per meal) have a significantly increased risk of bloat. Raised bowls also increase the risk of bloat.

To decrease your Bulldog's chances of falling victim to bloat, feed him two or more meals a day, supplement with low fat table scraps, and do not moisten dog kibble that is preserved with citric acid.

Anal Sac Disease

Dogs of all breeds and of any age may encounter anal sac problems. The anal sacs (often mistakenly called "glands") are two round organs located on each side of the anus (at the 4 and 8 o'clock positions). They exude powerful, bad-smelling secretions that apparently are used to give other dogs mating and territorial information. Every time the dog defecates, some of this material is deposited. Dogs can also empty their sacs when they are scared or overexcited.

In general, human foods that should not be given to dogs include chocolate, onions, grapes/raisins, large amounts of garlic, and macadamia nuts.

Anal sacs can be the source of a variety of problems. For example, they can become infected with bacteria, a condition referred to as anal sacculitis. They can also become impacted or overfilled, which can lead to acute discomfort and infection. Finally, anal sacs can develop tumors or foreign bodies. Signs that your dog is encountering anal sac problems include:

- Scooting the rear end along the ground
- Chewing or licking the tail base
- Clamping the tail down over the anus
- Reluctance to sit
- Difficulty passing feces

- Redness or swelling in the area; perhaps even an open, draining sore

Obese dogs have more trouble draining their anal sacs properly than other dogs, and this inability only leads to further problems. However, an impacted anal gland must be expressed (squeezed) to remove the offending material. Some people recommend routinely emptying the anal sacs as a regular part of the grooming routine.

Dogs with a history of anal sac problems may be candidates for surgical removal, which is the only way to permanently solve the problem. Because your dog doesn't really "need" them, this is a pretty benign procedure, although it requires general anesthesia, which always carries some degree of risk. If possible, schedule the surgery at the same time as some other, necessary surgery.

Did You Know?

Some dogs are born with anal canals that do not close properly and drain foul-smelling fluid as the dog walks around. These dogs are definite candidates for surgery.

Vomiting

Dogs vomit more easily than humans because of the way they have evolved. (They'll eat anything.) Vomiting is not a disease but a sign of any one of a number of problems. In many cases, it's a dietary indiscretion and nothing at all to worry about. Sometimes, however, it can be extremely serious. Vomiting up to once a week may be normal for some dogs. If vomiting continues for more than one day, call your vet.

Diarrhea

Like vomiting, diarrhea can be trivial or very serious. It is often a sign of intestinal disease. If diarrhea continues for more than a day, call your vet.

Bloody Stools

Bloody stool can signify a variety of problems. In general, black or tarry stools suggest bleeding from high up in the digestive tract, such as that produced by a stomach ulcer. Redder stools indicate a problem lower down. If the stools have red blotches or streaks, the problem is most likely in the large intestine. However, keep in mind that even food coloring or a change in diet can affect stool color. Observe the stool carefully and take a sample to the vet. Bleeding anywhere in the body can be serious.

CANINE EMERGENCIES

What seems to be a minor health problem can become a major

emergency rather quickly. Dogs, especially Bulldogs, are stoic about pain, and often by the time we notice something is wrong, it is already very wrong. If any health emergencies should occur, be sure to contact your vet immediately.

Poisons

There are so many plants, drugs, and cleaning products that are poisonous to dogs, it's impossible to list them all in a book of this size. However, for a complete listing of toxic plants and other vital information, visit the ASPCA's website at www.aspca.org.

The following descriptions are some of the more common poisonous substances for dogs.

Acetaminophen

While helpful to humans, dogs cannot process acetaminophen (Tylenol, Nyquil, etc.), and ingestion affects the liver and red blood cells. A toxic dose is 45 mg per pound of body weight—about six 375 mg capsules for a 50-pound (23 kg) Bulldog. Signs of poisoning include depression, vomiting, blood in the urine or feces, and brown or blue mucous membranes. Death can occur in 18 to 36 hours. If your dog has swallowed Tylenol, induce vomiting and get him to the vet, where gastric lavage, intravenous fluids, oxygen, vitamin C, and activated charcoal will be administered.

Chocolate

Neither chocolate nor the wrapper it comes in is good for your dog. Chocolate has a high fat content and contains caffeine and theobromine, which stimulate the nervous system and can be toxic. Signs of chocolate toxicity include restlessness, hyperactivity, muscle twitching, increased urination, and panting. Because chocolate is high in fat, it can cause gastrointestinal upset like vomiting, diarrhea, or pancreatitis.

If your dog gets into the chocolate box, call your vet. Most dogs recover quickly. Although not all kinds of chocolate are equally poisonous, you should still make sure that your Bulldog does not have access to any of them to avoid a potential problem.

Fireworks

It should be obvious that fireworks are extremely dangerous to dogs. Not only will a curious pet attempt to sniff lit fireworks,

Poison Control

If you think your pet has been poisoned, call your vet or the ASPCA National Animal Poison Control Center at (900) 443-0000 immediately. The charge is billed directly to the caller's phone. You can also call (888) 4ANI-HELP ((888) 426-4435), billed to the caller's credit card only. Follow-up calls can be made for no additional charge by dialing (888) 299-2973.

Your Canine First Aid Kit

Your canine first-aid kit should include the following items:

- **Antibiotic Ointment:** For minor skin infections.
- **Benadryl (either liquid or capsule):** For insect stings and allergies. Use 1 milligram per pound of dog (up to 50 mg).
- **Cotton Balls or Cotton Batting:** For cleaning ears and applying ointment.
- **Eye Wash:** For irritated eyes.
- **Hydrogen Peroxide:** To induce vomiting. Use 1 teaspoon every 15 minutes until it works.
- **Ipecac Syrup:** To induce vomiting. Use 1 teaspoon per 20 pounds (9kg) of dog every four to six hours.
- **Kaopectate:** For diarrhea. Use one spoonful for each 20 pounds (9 kg) of dog every four hours.
- **Pain Reliever:** If you don't have a prescription, you can probably get by safely with buffered aspirin. Most Bulldogs suffer no ill effects from it. Use one tablet every eight hours.
- **Petroleum Jelly:** To protect and lubricate his nose; also to lubricate the rectal thermometer.
- **Rectal Thermometer:** Get one made for dogs. Lubricate the thermometer with petroleum jelly and insert gently; hold for about two to three minutes. Be sure you hang onto the end, as you don't want it disappearing. Normal temperature for most dogs ranges from 100.5°F to 101°F (38°C to 38.3°C).
- **Styptic Powder:** To stop bleeding from inadvertent cuts during nail trimming.

which can cause severe facial burns, but even unlit fireworks are deadly if ingested. They contain poisons like potassium nitrate and heavy metals like mercury. If your dog ingests fireworks, he may have to be hospitalized.

Potpourri

As much as many of us enjoy brewing up some potpourri, it is dangerous to curious dogs, especially puppies. Potpourri contains toxic essential oils and detergents. Signs of potpourri poisoning may include burns on the skin or mouth, lack of appetite, drooling, vomiting, difficulty breathing, and weakness.

If your dog has been poisoned by potpourri, bathe him in lukewarm water and flush out his eyes if needed. If he ingested it, try giving him some milk or water and immediately take him to the vet.

Snakebite

The following are some signs that your dog has been bitten by a poisonous snake:

When a dog has an inflamed or infected ear, it hurts. This makes it harder to administer the soothing medication he needs, so you'll need to be careful and patient. Before you start, have the medication ready and the cap off. Try to hold the dog's head still with one hand and give the medication with the other. If you need to hold the ear open, be very gentle. Your dog will probably flinch when the medication goes in, so be prepared.

Most ear medication comes in a container with a long tube. Don't cram the tube into the ear; just hold it to the opening of the ear canal and squeeze gently. Rub the base of the ear to distribute the medicine all the way in.

- Lethargy
- Vomiting
- Diarrhea
- Excessive salivation
- Swelling and fang marks at the area of the bite
- Shock

If your dog is bitten, seek immediate veterinary care. Identify the snake if possible, but don't go crawling around in the bushes after it. Keep the dog quiet and immobilize the bitten part, trying to keep it below heart level. You may use a constricting bandage (not a tourniquet) if you are careful not to cut off the blood flow.

Wounds and Bleeding

If the wound is comparatively minor (no major bleeding), first remove debris and any foreign objects stuck in the wound. If you have clippers, cut the hair away from the wound site and clean the area with a cleansing solution. If soap is all you have, use that, but don't use hydrogen peroxide because it can damage the tissue. To control bleeding, apply direct pressure with a clean bandage and raise the bleeding portion higher than the rest of the body if possible.

If there is a lot of bleeding, do your best to get it under control and immediately rush your dog to the veterinarian.

Inability to Breathe

Dogs who have stopped breathing may respond to CPR. When performing CPR (cardiopulmonary resuscitation), you are giving your dog artificial respiration and chest compressions to get his heart going at the same time. If possible, it's best to have two people working: one for the breathing and one for the heart. Of course, that's not always possible. The chances of its success aren't great, but it is better than nothing.

CPR works using the ABC method: airway, breathing, and circulation.

Airway and Breathing

Lay the dog on his side on a flat surface. Breathing usually stops before the heart does. Sometimes people begin CPR on a dog who is actually breathing fine on his own, so it's vital to check before you start. It is actually dangerous to perform CPR on an animal who is breathing. A rising and falling chest indicates breathing is occurring. Dogs suffering from lack of oxygen have bluish gums.

If the dog is not breathing, *check the airway*. It may be blocked by a foreign object or vomit. To clear the airway, lay the dog on his side and gently tilt the head backward (if there is no neck trauma). If the airway is blocked, draw the tongue out. If that doesn't dislodge the object, sweep for foreign objects with your fingers or use pliers. (This is not recommended for humans, but it is okay with dogs.) If that doesn't work, try the Heimlich maneuver.

If your Bulldog is not breathing, gently pull his tongue out just a bit. Close the mouth by holding your hands around the muzzle, and tilt his head just a little to open the airway. Then, perform mouth-to-snout resuscitation. Breathe into the dog's nose four or five times, blowing just hard enough to see the chest expand. Check to see if your Bulldog is breathing. If he is still not breathing, keep trying until help arrives. You should give about 20 breaths a minute.

Circulation

To check the pulse, place your hand on the left side of the chest and feel for a heartbeat.

To work on the circulation, put your Bulldog on his back. (Most dogs should be placed on their sides, but barrel-chested dogs, like Bulldogs, need a different technique.) Use a hard surface to make the chest compressions more effective. Kneel next to the dog and place your cupped hands on top of each other over the ribs where the point of elbow meets the chest.

Transporting an Injured Bulldog

The best way to move your injured dog depends partly on his temperament and partly on the nature of the injury. If possible, put a muzzle on the dog before attempting to move him. Even the gentlest dog can bite when injured and frightened.

If you suspect a problem with the back or neck, put the dog on a board to reduce the possibility of further injury.

For Dogs Under 30 Pounds (13kg)

If your Bulldog is a puppy or unusually small and there is no back injury, pick him up and carry him, cradling his body. (Try to prevent kicking.) Wrap him in a blanket and hold the injured side against your body. Very young dogs can also be carried in a box or pet carrier.

For Dogs Over 30 Pounds (13 kg)

If you have help, place the dog in a blanket and have each person carry one end like a stretcher. If you have no help, you'll just have to tough it out and carry the dog to the car. You can do it.

Many dog owners are exploring the world of alternative therapies.

Compress the chest about 3 inches one and a half to two times per second (five compressions for each breath). Get the dog to a vet as soon as you can.

Heatstroke

Bulldogs are in great danger of heatstroke. Heatstroke can occur any time the temperature rises above 70°F (21°C). Dogs cannot perspire except on the pads of their feet, and that's just not very efficient. Their only other method of heat exchange is panting. Panting allows the dog to move large volumes of warm air away from the interior body to the outside. At the same time, that air moves over a wet tongue that is well-supplied with blood vessels. This also helps cool the blood. Still, dogs aren't tropical animals, and heat and humidity win out over a wet tongue. The hotter it is, the faster your dog has to pant.

This is one reason why dogs should never be left in the car in warm weather, even for a few minutes.

Heatstroke is easy to prevent. Make sure your Bulldog always has access to cool, fresh water, especially outdoors. Don't leave him outside in the heat in a shadeless area for even a short period. Exercise him only during the cooler periods of the day. If you go outside together, you might want to fill a kiddie pool with water so that he can refresh himself under your watchful eye.

Signs of heatstroke include panting, weakness, and incoordination. The dog may even look panicky and wild. His gums may be graying or dark red rather than healthy pink. Vomiting, diarrhea, seizures, and death may follow. If you suspect heatstroke, drench your Bulldog with cool (not cold) water. If his body temperature is over 105°F (40°C), he will require hospitalization and intravenous fluids. At that temperature, he is unable to get sufficient oxygen to his body tissues, and brain damage can occur.

CONVENTIONAL MEDICATION

From time to time I guarantee that your Bulldog will need some medication. Most often, your vet will give directions for its proper administration, but here are some general guidelines.

Dispensing Medication

Make sure you throw out any old medicine. In other words, when in doubt, throw it out!

Use all of the antibiotics your vet prescribes for your dog, even if you think the dog is better and doesn't need them anymore. Also, don't save them in the hope that you can use them on another dog if that one becomes sick. Antibiotics are not necessarily interchangeable. Also, follow the directions on the label and don't mix medications without checking with your vet first. The medication should be stored in its original container. Carefully observe your Bulldog for adverse reactions to any medication.

Liquids

Use a syringe if possible (without the needle, of course). You can get one from your vet. Squirt the medication into the back of the dog's mouth. Tuck the syringe neatly down the "cheek pocket" of the dog's mouth, and hold the jaws closed with the lips firmly together. Don't cram it down his throat, because you might get the medication into his lungs by mistake. Keep his head tilted upward.

Skunked!

Skunks not only smell terrible, but their secretions are extremely irritating to your dog's eyes. However, because skunks are nocturnal animals, keeping your dog in at night will prevent the problem. If your dog does get sprayed, you're in for a bit of a struggle. Of course, you'll have to wash the dog to get the scent off. Ordinary shampoos won't do the trick, though, and the wetter the dog gets, the worse he will smell. Run to the pet supply store and get a commercial anti-skunk remedy, or if it's the middle of night, as is likely, make your own anti-skunk medication using a quart of 3 percent hydrogen peroxide, 1/2 cup (118 ml) of baking soda, and 1 teaspoon of liquid soap. Wet the dog and rub in the mixture, leaving it on for three or four minutes. Repeat several times. Keep the stuff out of the dog's eyes. If you use peroxide, your Bulldog may bleach out until new hair growth comes in.

By the way, the traditional remedies like tomato juice or vinegar really don't work very well.

After giving the oral medication, stroke the throat gently.

Pills

If the medication can be given with food, wrap it in a piece of cheese and let him swallow it. If not, open his mouth and place the pill as far down his throat as possible.

ALTERNATIVE THERAPIES

Conventional veterinary medicine is no longer your only option, and many dog owners are exploring the new world of alternative therapies. According to Veterinary Pet Insurance, pet health insurance policies may cover all of the following alternative treatments if they are prescribed for a covered illness or injury and if they are administered by, or under the supervision of, a veterinarian.

Herbal Medications

Herbalism is of growing interest to dog owners who are looking for alternatives to Western medications. There are several approaches to the study of herbs, among them traditional Chinese medicine, Western herbalism, and Ayurvedic medicine, which originated in India and the Middle East. Although each branch of herbal medicine has a slightly different emphasis, all work by helping the body maintain its own health. This approach is in contradistinction to conventional Western medicine, which has traditionally operated by focusing on the disease process rather than on wellness, although things are changing.

Using herbs as medicine is not necessarily a do-it-yourself approach. Herbalism is a complex science, like conventional medicine, and best results are obtained when you visit a qualified veterinary herbalist. Many such practitioners also have a degree in veterinary medicine.

No one should approach herbal medication as a "quick fix." Most herbs act more slowly than do the potent drugs that partly derive from them. Several days may pass before the patient sees improvement. Nor are herbs some kind of "wonder drug" that will magically eliminate all of your pet's diseases. They are simply a method of treatment. Not every one will work on every disease, and some diseases have no cures at all, herbal or otherwise. In addition, many herbs lack the purity of laboratory-tested

Semi-sweet and baking chocolate are much more toxic than white or milk chocolate. About 12 ounces (355 ml) of semi-sweet chocolate will cause severe problems in the nervous system of the average Bulldog, while only four 1-ounce (30 ml) squares of baking chocolate can cause serious damage.

medications, and the dosages are not so precise.

That doesn't mean, however, that herbs are of no use. They can often alleviate pain and relieve symptoms. In some cases, they can effect a cure. In other words, they have exactly the same properties as conventional medications. Too often people use both herbs and drugs to treat their dog's symptoms and are then disappointed and surprised to find out that the disease itself remains. It is always important to remember that treating a symptom and treating the underlying condition do not necessarily call for the same herbal or drug regimen.

Dosages

Just as with conventional medications, herbal dosages vary from case to case. Luckily, however, herbs are much more forgiving in this regard than are Western-style drugs. In most cases, you can administer doses to your pet roughly in proportion to the recommended human dose. (In other words, give a 50-pound dog [22.7 kg] one half as much as you would give a 100-pound [45 kg] person.) However, since dogs have a faster metabolic rate than people, you may want to increase initial dosages to an effective level. It's generally safe to do this in 10 percent increments, up to 50 percent over the recommended starting dose. Again, this is something to work out with your animal herbalist.

Herbs

Here are some of the most popular herbs and their common usages:
- Red Clover (*Trifolium pratense*): Skin problems, swollen lymph nodes
- Oregon Grape (*Mahonia aquifolium*): Anti-inflammatory; antimicrobial
- Yucca (*Achillea millefolium*): Reduces inflammation
- Echinacea or Coneflower (*Echinacea spp.*): Boosts the immune system
- Sage (*Salvia officinalis*): Anti-microbial
- Ginkgo (*Ginkgo biloba*): Helps the urinary tract
- Licorice (*Glycyrrhiza glabra*): Anti-inflammatory
- Raspberry Leaf (*Rubus idaeus*): Helps conjunctivitis and is an astringent
- Nettle (*Urtica spp.*): Helps conjunctivitis and dermatitis; provides vitamins and minerals
- Dandelion (*Taraxacum officinale*): Diuretic; provides vitamins and minerals
- Slippery Elm (*Ulmus fulva*): Helps relieve gastrointestinal or urinary infections
- Cayenne (*Capsicum spp*): Helps circulation
- Skullcap (*Scutellaria spp*): Helps anxiety, relieves pain
- Aloe Vera (*Aloe spp.*): Promotes healing
- Fennel (*Foeniculum vulgare*): Helps indigestion and flatulence
- Chamomile (*Matricaria recutita*): Helps indigestion and flatulence
- Burdock (*Arctium lappa*): Helps seborrhea

Most herbalists also recommend that your dog take a break from herbal medication two days a week.

Herbal Diversity

Herbs act in a variety of ways, just as conventional medications do. Some are antimicrobial and help kill bacteria and fungi in the body. Others act as astringents and promote skin and bowel health. Some are sedatives, and some are diuretics. Some promote wellness of the cardiovascular tract. Some are anti-inflammatory, and some are carminatives, helping the digestive system function at its optimum level. Some help the entire immune system. Some promote healing. No brief survey can adequately describe the varied benefits of herbal medication, but it is something worthwhile for dog owners to research.

Herbal medications come in many forms. Probably the most useful is the dried bulk form. Some of these can be added directly to your dog's food. Storage time varies from herb to herb, and a lot depends on the way the herb is preserved. Read labels carefully, and don't try to store too much.

Overdoses of herbal medications can be toxic, just as with conventional medications. Signs of overdose

When to Get to the Vet

Astute owners know when it's time to get professional help for their Bulldogs. The following signs indicate veterinary care is needed:

- Heart or respiratory trouble (difficulty breathing, blue or white gums, near-drowning)
- Trauma (broken bone, cut exposing a bone, heavy bleeding that cannot be stopped, eye injury, fight with a wild or unvaccinated animal, bullet or arrow wound, struck by car, puncture wounds, head trauma, snake bite, broken tooth, fall, facial swelling, electric shock)
- Exposure to a poison
- Heat stroke or fever of 104°F (40°C) or higher
- Gastrointestinal distress (straining to eliminate, bloat, vomiting blood, uncontrolled vomiting, choking, swallowing of a foreign object, bloody diarrhea, tarry feces, protruding rectum)
- Problems with the nervous system (extreme lethargy, collapse, seizures, tilted head, staggering, continuous pain)
- Inability to bear weight on one or more feet
- Continual sneezing or coughing
- Crying when picked up or touched

include vomiting, diarrhea, and itching. Simply because something is herbal doesn't mean that it cannot, at the same time, be dangerous in large doses or for certain animals. Comfrey, for example, contains a fair amount of pyrrolizidine alkaloids, which can cause liver damage in some individuals. Red clover is rich in the anti-clotting compound coumarin, which is contraindicated in dogs with clotting disorders. Other herbs contain such potentially dangerous substances as anthraquinones, saponins, sterols, tannins, and volatile oils. Never casually dose your dog with herbs any more than you would dose him with a prescription drug. Your dog may have a condition that would make such a dosage dangerous. Consult an expert first.

Please don't collect herbs in the wild. It's easy to get varieties confused, and some native plants are becoming extremely rare because they have been heavily collected. Buy your herbal medication commercially and always on the advice of an experienced practitioner.

Homeopathy

Homeopathy has become an important part of legitimate veterinary practice. As a science, it is about 200 years old, but it has been practiced as a folk medicine for centuries. Today there are 1,350 recognized homeopathic remedies. The "discoverer" of homeopathy was Samuel Hahnemann, a German doctor who found that quinine, the medicine used at the time to cure malaria, actually caused malarial symptoms when given to a healthy person.

Homeopathy works on a simple, interesting principle: "Like cures like." To cure an illness, you give the patient a very small, diluted amount of a substance that in large amounts would produce symptoms similar to the target disease. The body responds by re-setting its systems to heal itself. The major philosophical difference between homeopathy and conventional Western medicine (which homeopaths call allopathy) is that traditional medicine usually works by introducing a completely different or foreign substance into the body to treat an illness. Homeopaths believe that this can cause more harm than good because it forces the body to deal with two problems rather than one while giving the body nothing to stimulate it to heal. Homeopaths feel that most Western medication merely eliminates symptoms; it doesn't cure

More About Homeopathy

All veterinary homeopaths have received traditional veterinary training and hold a veterinarian's license. They have also completed 128 hours of instruction in approved courses, have passed two exams, and have accepted four cases they plan to treat holistically. To find a homeopath near you, check the American Holistic Veterinary Medical Association at www.ahvma.org.

the patient. And because one disease can cause many symptoms, homeopaths also believe that Western medicine tends to overmedicate by treating the products of the disease (the symptoms) rather than the disease itself. This can make the disease worse rather than better. (The classic argument for this belief is the administration of corticosteroids for skin problems. The cure can be much worse than the original disease.)

Homeopathic remedies come in pellet or liquid form. If you are using pellets and have no further directions, the right dose for most Bulldogs is four to five pellets. Smaller Bulldogs can get by with three. Most homeopathic remedies have a sweet taste, and dogs appear to enjoy them.

"Homeopathy is a very safe method of treatment for illness. Still, nothing is completely without risk. Too many people tend to use homeopathy as a last resort, and they don't give such remedies until the dog is already very, very sick. Most of these people are inexperienced in the art of homeopathy and also may give the wrong dose. A dose that is "almost" right is very wrong in homeopathy."

Homeopathy, an alternative method of healing, operates on the principle that "like cures like."

Never substitute homeopathic home care for qualified veterinary practice. In particular, don't attempt homeopathic remedies for an emergency condition unless you are on the road to the vet at the same time. Finally, always check with a homeopathic vet before administering homeopathic remedies designed for human beings. The dosages and applications may differ.

Flower Essence Therapy

Edward Bach developed this branch of alternative medicine in England early in the 20th century. Today there are about 50,000 active practitioners of the art worldwide. Although there are 38 different combinations of flower essences in Bach's pharmacopeia (and more than 200 other blends developed since then), the best known today is Bach's special blend of five flower essences. It is produced and sold under various names such as Rescue Remedy and Five Flower Formula. This particular decoction is widely marketed for its calming effect on nervous and stressed dogs.

The theory behind flower essence therapy is called resonance, and healers caution that they work best when the essence you select matches the core emotional challenges the dog faces (if you can figure out what they are). Treating only surface symptoms is futile. Nor are they designed to be a cure for physical ailments; instead, they are intended for psychological and emotional problems that can develop into physical distress. Although flower essences are usually preserved in brandy, you can also use cider vinegar.

Flower essences are usually administered in a dose of four drops four times a day. They can be rubbed into the gums or added to some bread and fed to the dog. Flower essence therapy requires frequent application, as its effects seem transient. It is often combined with other kinds of therapy, particularly herbs and essential oils.

Chiropractic Therapy

Dogs who develop bone and joint problems may benefit from a visit to the veterinary chiropractor. Chiropractic treatment is not a replacement for conventional care, but it can be a valuable addition to it. Your Bulldog can visit either a veterinarian or a chiropractor for these services, but both need special training in animal chiropractic care. Such a practitioner would be licensed by the American Veterinary Chiropractic Association.

Although the benefits of chiropractic care are many, chiropractors can't work miracles. They will not be able to cure hip or elbow dysplasia, for instance. However, by carefully manipulating vertebrae, they can prevent minor spinal problems from turning into more serious ones.

Chiropractors feel for irregularities (subluxations) between vertebrae and adjust them, restoring correct vertebral alignment. Chiropractic care seems especially beneficial for disk problems and may help prevent surgery or offer valuable aftercare. Even conformation dogs, obedience dogs, and canine athletes like agility dogs can benefit from chiropractic treatment by elevating their performance to the very best level possible.

Acupuncture

Acupuncture is an age-old Chinese art that was originally designed for animals. It is ideal for dogs with arthritis, spondylosis, and hip dysplasia—in fact, most musculoskeletal disorders. It has also been used successfully in dogs with cancer, allergies, and problems in the nervous and circulatory systems.

Acupuncture involves the gentle insertion of fine needles, but dogs seldom need to be sedated for treatment. Most of them don't even notice it.

No one is really sure how or why acupuncture works. Traditional acupuncturists believe it channels the flow of Qi, a Chinese word for energy, through certain "body paths" known as meridians. Western-trained acupuncturists have a different theory. They note that the acupoints, or sites of acupuncture, usually have a thinner epidermis than surrounding tissues, and each one contains a lymph vessel, arteriole, and vein, in addition to a bundle of nerve fibers. They believe that the needles stimulate the central and automatic nervous systems, which release endorphins that lessen the perception of pain. Other acupoints may release cortisol, a natural steroid. Of course, either explanation may be true, or there may be another reason altogether.

Acupuncture has undergone further refinement with the development of electroacupuncture, a practice in which traditionalneedle acupuncture is combined with a microcurrent of electricity.

Physical Therapy

Many dogs benefit from physical therapy after surgery or when plagued with a chronic condition. Most dogs can begin physical therapy within 48 hours after surgery, and sessions run twice weekly for four to six weeks.

A canine physical therapist may be a veterinarian, licensed veterinary technician, or licensed human physical therapist with special training in canine therapy. If you find a regular physical therapist who is certified to practice on animals, make sure she will work in partnership with your vet for the best outcome for your dog.

Types of physical therapy include:

- *Hydrotherapy:* Provides an almost weightless environment to improve range of motion and muscle strength, usually by means of an underwater treadmill. These are still rare, but expect their use to increase.

- *Therapeutic ultrasound:* Conducts high-frequency sound waves to muscles to reduce pain and muscle spasms. It also enhances collagen production, increases blood flow, and speeds wound healing.

- *Neuromuscular stimulation:* Uses electrical stimulation to help dogs regain muscle function and improve range of motion.

- *Passive range of motion therapies:* Involve manipulating the dog's limbs and joints in an effort to stimulate blood flow and increase range of motion in weak or paralyzed limbs.

- *Therapeutic exercises:* Build muscle, recover balance, and strengthen the cardiovascular system.

SENIOR DOGS

Senior dogs often have special health needs and are more prone diseases, such as cancer and arthritis, than are younger dogs. To help keep your senior in the best of health, it's important to establish a great relationship with your vet and make sure your senior gets a checkup at least twice a year. Your Bulldog's teeth are especially in need of extra attention. Keep brushing them daily, and get them professionally cleaned as often as your veterinarian recommends.

Many older dogs have built up plenty of immunity against various diseases. Talk with your vet about stopping vaccinations or reducing their frequency.

Your senior dog will have more trouble processing food than will a younger dog. Help him out by buying top quality food, with plenty of protein. (Only seniors with poor kidney function should be on a low protein food). In fact, studies have shown that a healthy senior dog requires 50 percent more protein than a young adult! However, don't overfeed him. Obesity is a major problem in Bulldogs—especially the older fellows. Obesity will shorten his life.

If your senior has arthritis, it's important to support him with dietary supplements recommended by your veterinarian. And just because your dog is old and arthritic doesn't mean he doesn't need his exercise. He does, for both mental and physical reasons. He may not go fast, and it may take him a while to "warm up," but a walk two or three times a day will benefit his spirit, weight, and overall health.

Senior dogs have special needs that should be monitored and addressed by a qualified veterinarian.

Older dogs tend to chill easily, so keep him warm and comfortable and out of any drafty areas. Soft orthopedic beds are particularly appreciated.

Please continue to make your older dog a part of your life. Don't exclude him now. You owe your senior Bulldog as much care now as you did when he was a playful pup. This wise old philosopher has much to teach all of us about the dignity and trials of aging. We would do well to listen.

ORGANIZATIONS

American Kennel Club (AKC)
5580 Centerview Drive
Raleigh, NC 27606
Telephone: (919) 233-9767
Fax: (919) 233-3627
E-mail: info@akc.org
www.akc.org

Association of Pet Dog Trainers
(APDT)
150 Executive Center Drive
Box 35
Greenville, SC 29615
Telephone: (800) PET-DOGS
Fax: (864) 331-0767
E-mail: information@apdt.com
www.apdt.com

Canadian Kennel Club (CKC)
89 Skyway Avenue, Suite 100
Etobicoke, Ontario M9W 6R4
Telephone: (416) 675-5511
Fax: (416) 675-6506
E-mail: information@ckc.ca
www.ckc.ca

Delta Society
875 124th Ave NE, suite 101
Bellevue, WA 98005
Telephone: (425) 226-7357
Fax: (425) 235-1076
E-mail: info@deltasociety.org
www.deltasociety.org

The Bulldog Club of America
Secretary: Kathy Moss
E-mail: mossrose@ev1.net
www.thebca.org

The Kennel Club
1 Clarges Street
London W1J 8AB
Telephone: 0870 606 6750
Fax: 0207 518 1058
www.the-kennel-club.org.uk

United Kennel Club (UKC)
100 E. Kilgore Road
Kalamazoo, MI 49002-5584
Telephone: (269) 343-9020
Fax: (269) 343-7037
E-mail: pbickell@ukcdogs.com
www.ukcdogs.com

INTERNET RESOURCES

The Bulldog Club of America
(www.thebca.org)
This website is dedicated to the
propagation of the Bulldog
and also provides information
on breeder referrals, rescue
contacts, and specialty shows.

**The Bulldog Information
Library**
(www.bulldoginformation.com)
With the ability to be viewed in
six different languages, this
comprehensive website provides
information on health care,
raising, andpurchasing Bulldogs.
It also includes links to
international Bulldog clubs and
breeders.

PUBLICATIONS

BOOKS

Adamson, Eve. *The Guide to
Owning a Bulldog.* Neptune City:
T.F.H. Publications, Inc., 2004.

Brearley, Joan M. *The Book of the
Bulldog.* Neptune City: T.F.H.
Publications, Inc., 1985.

Fisher, Betty. Caninestein:
Unleashing the Genius in Your Dog.
New York City: HarperCollins
Publishers, 1997.

Fisher, Betty, and Suzanne Delzio,
So Your Dog's Not Lassie. New York
City: HarperCollins Publishers,
1998.

Fischer, Renaldo, and Michele St.
George. *The Shaman's Bulldog: A
Love Story.* New York City:
Warner Books Inc., 1996.

Hoflin. *The Bulldog Annual.*
Wheat Ridge: Hoflin Publishing,
Inc., 1993-2002.

Maggitti, Phil, and Tana
Hakanson Monslave. *Bulldogs: A
Complete Pet Owner's Manual.*
Hauppauge: Barron's
Educational Series, 1997.

Thomas, Chris. *Bulldogs Today.*
Vermont: Trafalgar Square Books,
2000.

Williams, Hank and Carol. *A New
Owner's Guide to Bulldogs.*
Neptune City: T.F.H.
Publications, Inc., 1998.

MAGAZINES

AKC *Family Dog*
American Kennel Club
260 Madison Avenue
New York, NY 10016
Telephone: (800) 490-5675
E-mail: familydog@akc.org
www.akc.org/pubs/familydog

AKC *Gazette*
American Kennel Club
260 Madison Avenue
New York, NY 10016
Telephone: (800) 533-7323
E-mail: gazette@akc.org
www.akc.org/pubs/gazette

Dog & Kennel
Pet Publishing, Inc.
7-L Dundas Circle
Greensboro, NC 27407
Telephone: (336) 292-4272
Fax: (336) 292-4272
E-mail: info@petpublishing.com
www.dogandkennel.com

Dog Fancy
Subscription Department
P.O. Box 53264
Boulder, CO 80322-3264
Telephone: (800) 365-4421
E-mail: barkback@dogfancy.com
www.dogfancy.com

Dogs Monthly
Ascot House
High Street, Ascot,
Berkshire SL5 7JG
United Kingdom
Telephone: 0870 730 8433
Fax: 0870 730 8431
E-mail:
admin@rtcassociates.freeserve.co.uk
www.corsini.co.uk/dogsmonthly

ANIMAL WELFARE GROUPS AND RESCUE ORGANIZATIONS

**American Humane Association
(AHA)**
63 Inverness Drive East
Englewood, CO 80112
Telephone: (303) 792-9900
Fax: 792-5333
www.americanhumane.org

RESOURCES

American Society for the
Prevention of Cruelty to
Animals
(ASPCA)
424 E. 92nd Street
New York, NY 10128-6804
Telephone: (212) 876-7700
www.aspca.org

Royal Society for the
Prevention
of Cruelty to Animals (RSPCA)
Telephone: 0870 3335 999
Fax: 0870 7530 284
www.rspca.org.uk

The Humane Society of the
United States (HSUS)
2100 L Street, NW
Washington DC 20037
Telephone: (202) 452-1100
www.hsus.org

VETERINARY RESOURCES

Academy of Veterinary
Homeopathy (AVH)
P.O. Box 9280
Wilmington, DE 19809
Telephone: (866) 652-1590
Fax: (866) 652-1590
E-mail: office@TheAVH.org
www.theavh.org

American Academy of
Veterinary
Acupuncture (AAVA)
100 Roscommon Drive, Suite 320
Middletown, CT 06457
Telephone: (860) 635-6300
Fax: (860) 635-6400
E-mail: office@aava.org
www.aava.org

American Animal Hospital
Association (AAHA)
P.O. Box 150899
Denver, CO 80215-0899
Telephone: (303) 986-2800
Fax: (303) 986-1700
E-mail: info@aahanet.org
www.aahanet.org/index.cfm

American Holistic Veterinary
Medical Association (AHVMA)
2218 Old Emmorton Road
Bel Air, MD 21015
Telephone: (410) 569-0795
Fax: (410) 569-2346
E-mail: office@ahvma.org
www.ahvma.org

American Veterinary Medical
Association (AVMA)
1931 North MeachamRoad
Suite 100
Schaumburg, IL 60173
Telephone: (847) 925-8070
Fax: (847) 925-1329
E-mail: avmainfo@avma.org
www.avma.org

British Veterinary
Association (BVA)
7 Mansfield Street
London
W1G 9NQ
Telephone: 020 7636 6541
Fax: 020 7436 2970
E-mail: bvahq@bva.co.uk
www.bva.co.uk

ABOUT THE AUTHOR

In her spare time (away from her animals), Diane Morgan is an assistant professor of philosophy and religion at Wilson College, Chambersburg, PA. She has authored numerous books on canine care and nutrition and has also written many breed books, horse books, and books on Eastern philosophy and religion. She is an avid gardener (and writes about that, too). Diane lives in Williamsport, Maryland with several dogs, two cats, some fish, and a couple of humans.

PHOTO CREDITS

Nylabone®

He **Plays** Hard.
He **Chews** Hard.

He's a **Nylabone**® Dog!
Your #1 choice for healthy chews & treats.

Nylabone proudly offers high-quality durable chews,
delicious edible treats, and fun, interactive toys for dogs of all sizes, shapes, and life stages.

Nylabone Products • P.O. Box 427, Neptune, NJ 07754-0427 • 1-800-631-2188 • Fax: 732-988-5466
www.nylabone.com • info@nylabone.com • For more information contact your sales representative or contact us at sales@tfh.com

A318